Highsmith

A Romance of the 1950s

Highsmith

A Romance of the 1950s

A Memoir

by

Marijane Meaker

Published in the United States by Cleis Press Inc., P.O. Box 14684, San Francisco, California 94114.

Printed in the United States.
Cover design: Scott Idleman
Text design: Karen Quigg
Cleis Press logo art: Juana Alicia
First Edition.
10 9 8 7 6 5 4 3 2

Library of Congress Cataloging-in-Publication Data

Meaker, Marijane, 1927-
    Highsmith : a romance of the 1950s / a memoir by Marijane Meaker. — 1st ed.
        p. cm.
    ISBN 1-57344-171-6 (alk. paper)
    1. Highsmith, Patricia, 1921-   . 2. Authors, American—20th century—Biography. 3. Lesbians—United States—Biography. 4. Meaker, Marijane, 1927-   . I. Title.
    PS3558.I366Z77 2003
    813'.54—dc21
    [B]

    2002154052

For Kit, there then and here now, with love.

One

L's was on a little side street in Greenwich Village, a dark, cozy lesbian bar.

It was the beginning of graciousness in the lesbian bar world. There was no evidence of Mafia ownership, no men in baggy double-breasted suits sporting pinkie rings guarding the door. In fact, no men were allowed. The bathroom was clean. The customers didn't seem to be divided so much into butch and femme. Most looked like young college girls, well-dressed and without the heavy makeup some habituées wore.

Hookers were often regular customers of gay bars; their butches waited for them there. But there was none of that in L's. The women behind the bar and at the door were welcoming. The music was mellow: Jeri Southern singing "You Better Go Now," and Frances Faye crooning "I'm Drunk with Love."

A handsome, dark-haired woman in a trench coat, drinking gin, stood at the bar, while around her there was the buzz that she was Claire Morgan!

She was better known in the outside world as Patricia Highsmith, author of *Strangers on a Train,* which had become an Alfred Hitchcock thriller in 1951.

But in L's, Pat was revered for her pseudonymous novel, *The Price of Salt,* which had been published in 1952 by Coward McCann. It was for many years the only lesbian novel, in either hard or soft cover, with a happy ending.

It stood on every lesbian bookshelf, along with classics like *The Well of Loneliness; We, Too, Are Drifting; Diana;* and *Olivia.*

Pat was thirty-eight, six years older than I was, and an inveterate traveler. Perhaps I had never met her for that reason, for she liked going to gay bars, as I did, and as my partner did not.

This night I was alone, because Kit had brought work home from the office. A gay bar was like a club. It was a place where you could meet with old friends and make new ones. You would always find a familiar face there, or you would know the owner, and the bartender. There was always someone to talk with.

Pat had become my idol. Although we were both reviewed in Anthony Boucher's mystery column in the *New York Times,* she was published in hardcover by Harper Brothers. As Vin Packer, I was one of Gold Medal Books' mystery/suspense paperback "tough guys," and, as Ann Aldrich, a softcover reporter on lesbian life.

I somehow found the courage to go over and introduce myself.

Pat was tall and thin. Black, shoulder-length hair, with dark brown eyes. She looked like a combination of Prince Valiant and Rudolf Nureyev.

She was as different from the usual woman I was attracted to as night from day, and I think vice versa. We were probably both drawn to more feminine types, what used to be called "girly girls." But we were both writers and hearty drinkers. We had very little trouble establishing an immediate rapport. When a table became free, we sat down.

Pat smoked Gauloises and drank gin neat.

Her conversation was sometimes punctuated with German, a few phrases tossed in, always "bitte" for *please,* said in a kindly tone or an irritated one. I asked her about it and she told me she'd taught herself. Left-handed, she didn't respond well to teachers who tried to help her use her right hand. In the '30s when she was growing up, a south-paw was considered flawed. She finally found a solution and, on her own, copied sentences from a German language book over and over with her right hand.

She said she chose German because she already knew some French and Spanish. But as I got to know her better, I realized that it stemmed from a melancholy affection for the father she never really knew. His family were German immigrants. His name was Jay Plangman. Her mother had divorced him when Pat was a baby. At age twelve Pat met him briefly, but while I knew her, and I believe for all her life, she had no other meetings with him. For whatever reason, it seemed to be his decision. He was American born, but Pat seemed proud of the fact that there was German in her blood. Stanley Highsmith, her stepfather, had not impressed her as much as the biological one she could make into whatever image she chose.

That night Pat asked me if I liked to travel. Much later, I would remember that it was the first question she asked me about myself, a foreshadowing of things to come.

I told her I had been to London and France with my family when I was a kid, and to Europe again with friends in 1952 and 1954, but now I was grounded. I'd finally qualified for a professional apartment, sought after by the self-employed in the '50s, low rent, and rent controlled, a real prize in the postwar era. And I'd adopted five cats. I didn't mention Kit.

Pat said she did her best work in Europe, that she had tried Mexico, but her favorite places were France and Italy. It was her custom to set sail on a tramp steamer, taking whatever space there was at the last minute. It was the cheapest way to travel, she told me, and the only drawback was that she was given very short notice. She would receive a call that she was to be ready in five or six hours, and she would pack a duffel bag and her typewriter. Then she would settle into someplace like Marseille, where she would set up shop in a small hotel and work on her latest novel. From there she would visit Paris, Venice, Florence, Rome.

"How come you don't go to Germany?" I asked her. "You seem to love the language."

"The language is one thing, the place another. I don't like German food that much, and it's too expensive there."

We were shouting above the noise of a Friday night bar, overcrowded as all gay bars were in the days when they were the only place to socialize.

L's was a far cry from the usual tawdry place, and even though it was hard to hear each other we stayed on until closing.

I told her that when *I* wrote *my* lesbian novel, *Spring Fire,* a paperback published by Fawcett, it had to end unhappily. Paperbacks went through the mails and were scrutinized by postal censors. Nothing would be okayed that seemed to endorse a perverse way of life.

"My main character's name was Leda," I said. "She ended up in an insane asylum."

"Leda the Mad!" Pat laughed.

She said she'd been surprised when her book, written under the name Claire Morgan, was praised by lesbian readers because of its happy ending. She was pleased that it had become such a hit for that reason.

"But I never thought about it when I wrote it. I just told the story."

She said it had been inspired by a woman she waited on when she was working part-time in Macy's. There was something very compelling about the woman. Pat couldn't forget her. She'd copied her address from the sales slip. On her day off she took a bus to New Jersey, found the woman's house, and simply walked by it. That was all. The next day she came down with chicken pox, but as soon as she was able to sit up in bed, she began writing *The Price of Salt*.

At the cry "Last call!" we ordered another round, and finally it was time to go.

Pat said she'd just that afternoon returned from Mexico. She'd heard about L's from a friend. It was always word-of-mouth that brought us to the gay bars in those days.

"I'm glad I came," she said. "I haven't even unpacked or I'd invite you by for a nightcap."

"That's all I need, a nightcap," I laughed.

We were walking out the door. "I live on Irving Place, within walking distance," she said.

"I live nearby, too." I didn't add that I lived with someone. Kit was editing a book that had to be finished that night. But, knowing Kit, I realized she was glad to be spared a visit to a gay bar. She was very closeted, always afraid someone from the office would see her going in, or coming out. She was convinced straight people all knew which bars were gay.

Pat and I were standing in the street. She had taken my hand. I remember the smile on her face; she had a great smile.

"Will you have lunch with me tomorrow?" she asked me.

"I'd like that." Kit was going away: perfect timing.

"Do you know where Pete's Restaurant is?"

I knew it was on the street where she lived. I'd been to Pete's when I'd first moved to New York City. I went there because it was said O. Henry wrote many of his short stories there. I'd never wanted to be anything but a writer.

I agreed to meet Pat at Pete's, at noon.

"Good!" she said. "There's a friend of mine who'll join us."

I felt sick at the thought that she was with someone, too. But she was slow to let go of my hand, and after we walked away from each other, when I looked back, she did as well.

I strolled home, unbelievably sober, the way you stay sometimes no matter how much you've had to drink, because something changeful has happened.

Two

Pat was already seated when I arrived at Pete's. She stood up, as she always did for females, bowing slightly, and grinning.

"Meet my friend," she said, and a small, thin man got to his feet, too.

Pat told me, "This is José Garcia Villa." I would learn that she always said all three names, "and that's Freddy."

José shook my hand vigorously and a young man also at the table gave me a little two-fingered salute.

Freddy was a very handsome fellow, about eighteen or nineteen. José was fiftyish, a frail-looking Filipino-American poet with large bags under his eyes and a merry disposition.

I was barely settled next to Pat when José announced that Freddy and he had been "fluving" all morning, and were therefore very hungry.

"Fluving," he said, "is fucking with love. I just invented the word!"

Freddy had a great white smile, and he nodded vigorously.

We all ordered a pitcher of beer, and hamburgers, popular at Pete's with its sawdust floors and collegiate atmosphere.

Freddy was the only one not drinking. Before our hamburgers arrived, another pitcher of beer was put on the table.

Pat had brought with her José's new poetry collection, "with an introduction by Dame Edith Sitwell, no less."

"I bet you haven't even read it, Pat," José teased, as he autographed it for her.

"I can prove that I have," she said. "One of the poems I liked was the one with the line 'seventeen times I rose creating our child.'"

José held his head in mock agony. "That's one I hate! Ask yourself what kind of an idiot would be counting at a time like that?"

I knew immediately that I was going to enjoy this lunch. Not a small part of my pleasure came from the relief I felt that Pat hadn't brought a woman with her. Kit had gone to Bellport on Long Island early that morning, to work with a writer whose book she was editing. She would stay overnight.

Kit knew what a Highsmith fan I was. In a game of Truth once, when everyone had to say who they'd want to be if they had to be someone else, I'd actually said Patricia Highsmith.

That morning I'd explained to Kit I was late getting in the night before because I'd met Pat Highsmith. I added that I'd been asked to lunch by Pat, and Kit said, "Did you tell her about me?"

"Not yet."

"Not yet," Kit said sarcastically.

I knew she was furious. On her way out, she slammed our apartment door so hard it shook our windows.

That warm April afternoon at Pete's, José began quoting various poets: Blake, Cummings, Dickinson.

Freddy said nothing, only smiled. Apparently he knew his smile was one of his best features, for the moment he finished his hamburger he left the table.

"He's gone to brush his teeth!" José said with an adoring tone of voice. "He doesn't let any time pass after he's eaten."

Then José turned to Pat and said, "Speaking of teeth, is that a dentist's jacket? That looks like a dentist's coat."

Pat was wearing a white cotton jacket, a black turtleneck sweater, black men's pants (29w, 34l), and black loafers. The sweater was tucked in and her black leather belt featured a large silver belt buckle.

She told José that it wasn't a dentist's jacket. "But you're close. It's a *waiter's* jacket I bought in Marseille."

"Oh, I didn't mean it!" José's face was red.

"I don't care." Pat shrugged. "I know it looks like what it is. It's my purse. I carry everything in the pockets."

"Let me try it on," José said.

By now he and Pat were drinking shots of J & B scotch, to go with the beer, pitchers of which we'd already been through.

Freddy came back from brushing his teeth and tried the jacket on, too. Then I tried it on.

Pat said, "If you all really like it, I'll buy three when I go to Marseille."

"When will that be?" José asked.

"In a week or two. I have to wait until I can get a cabin."

I listened, downcast, while she told me she'd only returned to this country to attend to some business. She was going away again as soon as she could. In a hushed voice she said, "I'm sorry. I *am*."

Freddy and José were huddled together talking and giggling.

Pat looked directly at me. "Do you have a lover?"

"I'm at the end of a relationship," I lied.

I didn't want to lose Kit, but I didn't want to lose Pat, either, for whatever little time we could have together.

"Do *you* have someone?" I asked her.

She shook her head.

"Freddy wants to try the jacket on again," José said.

"Good, because I'll have to figure out the sizes!" Pat told him.

We were jumping up and down, laughing, taking great swallows of the beer, and talking all at one time.

Somewhere in the noise I heard Pat ask, "Will you have dinner with me?"

José heard it, too. "Let's *all* have dinner!" he said.

Freddy nodded happily.

"Where?" Pat said.

"Right here!" José said. "We don't have to move. It's four-thirty now. We'll stay right here!"

"Okay," Pat signaled to the waiter to bring another round.

"This place reminds me of the White Horse," José said, "and the White Horse reminds me of nights with Dylan. Someone read aloud my poem about his death. Please? It's on page 151." He pushed his book to the center of the table.

"Marijane?" Pat said.

José reached across and found the page. It was called "Death and Dylan Thomas."

First lines:

Gold, gong, of,
Genius:continual, fire:leger, nobler,

There was a comma after almost every word.

Pat explained later that José compared his method to Seurat's pointillism, where the points of color are as much a part of the medium as the technique of expression.

Amazed that I read the poem well, and that I still felt sober, I was delighted with the plan to stay. José and Freddy deflected the tension I felt whenever Pat spoke directly to me. I was more relaxed with them there. I knew Pat hadn't intended to have dinner with them, but she was easy with the idea. That was her way: to go along with what others wanted.

Pat had run out of Gauloises, and no place nearby sold French cigarettes. Her apartment building was just doors away on Irving Place. She asked me if I wanted to go there with her while she got a pack. I could also meet her cat, Spider.

"We'll be right back," she told José.

I still remember that walk. She took long steps, her shoulder-length black hair bobbing, one of her hands sunk into her trousers pocket. (Pat's pants were always neatly pressed; she ironed them herself.)

It was a warm spring afternoon, and there was an ice cream truck at the corner playing "Swanee."

Pat was singing along with the music, "how I love yah, how I love yah," with that silly grin of hers, as we went up the stone steps. She lived on the first floor, in the front.

I don't know who reached out first, once we got inside the door. A black cat was weaving its way in and out of our legs, chirping and mewing.

It was a while before we could speak.

"Do you mind José Garcia Villa and Freddy?"

"No, I don't." We were both whispering, as though we weren't alone.

"I'll get the Gauloises."

Pat opened a can of cat food for Spider. The apartment was one long room, very simply furnished, with a double bed; a small, kneehole desk with her portable Olympic typewriter on it; a square dining table; and six chairs. There was no television. Pat had already told me she never watched TV.

"José Garcia Villa isn't usually that silly," she said.

"Is he married? He mentioned his child in the poem."

"He's married, and he has two children. But he lives in his own apartment in the Village. He's Catholic; he can't get a divorce. That's probably what saves him: that he has to live with some sort of decorum. He's very involved in Filipino affairs."

The ice cream truck was playing "Swanee" over and over as we embraced.

By the time we pulled ourselves together and returned to Pete's, about forty minutes had passed.

The waiter handed Pat an envelope with money inside and a note saying, *Freddy doesn't feel well. Call before you leave the country. Love, José.*

We went back to Pat's, and much later we taxied to a restaurant on Bleecker Street called Aldo's.

It was always easier to eat in a gay restaurant. While not a lot of them were ever known for their food, young women were not turned away on a Saturday night if they were wearing pants. There was a welcoming ambiance, and most of us got to know the owners or the managers. Unlike gay *bars*, which were Mafia-run and often rude to their patrons, restaurants like Aldo's, the Fedora, and the Finale gave you support. All located in Greenwich Village, you felt comfortable in them. You could hold hands, sit close, and enjoy being treated like any other couple.

Lucky for me there was no one there who knew me or Kit.

Aldo's was ideal for two women who were just beginning to fall in love.

Three

I spent that Sunday nursing a hangover. Pat went off to Palisades, New York, for an overnight visit with her friend, the artist Polly Cameron, who also wrote and illustrated children's books.

Pat called me from there that afternoon, and asked me if I liked Paella Valenciana.

"I love it!" It had been years since I had carried an empty casserole from an apartment on Charles Street to a restaurant called Seville, on the corner of Charles and 10th. There it would be filled with paella. It had been years since I had hung out with butches so masculine they could not go to restaurants because they would not be accepted in either the men's or the women's bathrooms.

Pat said she knew of a wonderful restaurant specializing in paella, and she would like to take me to lunch at Seville.

I didn't tell her I knew about Seville. She sounded so pleased to have discovered it.

I said, "How about dinner, instead?" I didn't think I could face drinking in the daytime again.

"I can't wait that long, can you?" she asked.

"No." I couldn't.

"We'll have dinner, too. I'll cook."

"Okay," I said.

Although I had told her that I was still living with an ex, she never asked questions about Kit. It was no wonder, since I didn't mention Kit. I didn't want to think about Kit, or the consequences if I just kept agreeing to do whatever Pat wanted to do. It didn't occur to me that I would lose Kit. I would lie, talk myself out of blame, *something.*

In my seven years as a self-supporting freelance writer, I had never gone off schedule in the middle of a book. I had never indulged in boozy lunches, either.

But there I was clinking margarita glasses with Pat at noon the following day, then downing pitchers of sangria, the last lunch customers to leave Seville.

I was near the end of a suspense book called *The Girl on the Bestseller List.* It was about the murder of a Grace Metalious type, a best-selling woman novelist. My heroine had written a book like *Peyton Place,* and gained many enemies in her small town, who saw themselves in her characters. But she was not murdered by someone who hated her. She was done in by someone who loved her, and who had hoped to seduce her with a generous portion of Spanish fly, which was claimed to be a potent aphrodisiac. It was also a lethal poison in an overdose.

I didn't have to tell Kit what was happening to me. I didn't stay out all night, but I came in early Tuesday morning. Kit had to go to work in a few hours. I would sleep past noon.

My excuse to Kit was that while Patricia Highsmith fascinated me, she would be off to Europe very soon. She and I were just having a fling.

We had many gay male acquaintances who could countenance a good deal of infidelity, if the bond was strong. We knew no lesbians who could, and Kit was no exception.

"*She's* having a fling," Kit said. "*You're* head over heels in love with her!"

Two weeks later, Kit packed her bags and moved back to a small apartment she kept on Horatio Street.

I was nowhere near the drinker Pat was. I was used to drinking a lot, one night a weekend. Weeknights I didn't like to drink, because I always had more than I needed, and that would ruin writing for me the next day. I had always been a media hound, but the only TV I seemed to watch was the *Today Show* with Dave Garroway, which I turned on after Pat left, mornings. I had missed *Compulsion* with Orson Welles, still hadn't seen the new Broadway show *Sweet Bird of Youth,* nor gotten around yet to reading the latest works of Capote and James Jones. Forget about Castro's goodwill tour of the United States: I was behind in everything.

My book was stopped in its tracks. I could feel myself weakened physically by the alcohol. What I did to save myself was tell Pat that I was on a strict schedule, and could not meet for any more lunches. Then, while she thought I was writing, I did only a minimal amount of work. I spent most of the days sleeping, eating salads, drinking milkshakes, swallowing vitamins, in an attempt to recover for another evening of cocktails, wine with dinner, and brandy after.

Pat, meanwhile, was working on a book she called *The Two Faces of Janus.* It took place in Athens, Iraklion, Charria, Paris, and Marseille.

She never seemed to lose a day because of drinking the night before.

She would read parts of her novel to me while her very solemn black cat, Spider, sat beside her, looking up at her and listening as though she was instructing him in something.

Pat would lie across her double bed next to the window looking down on Irving Place. Over the bed hung a large and very startling oil portrait of Pat herself, her dark eyes glaring, her hair longer, face more drawn, mouth set grimly. It had been done in 1944 when Pat was twenty-three. Allela Cornell was the artist and a good friend of Pat's. She had killed herself in 1947.

Pat really enjoyed reading me new chapters. She would laugh hard at her own descriptions of characters she'd created. But again, Pat complained that she couldn't work well in America.

She said her best ideas came to her in foreign places.

"Some of my best titles come to me in this country," she said. "The idea for Tom Ripley came to me in Italy, but I got his name when I was driving up the West Side Drive, and saw a billboard for Ripley clothing. 'Tom Ripley,' I thought: 'the talented Tom Ripley.'"

She told me she used to get titles and characters' names driving from Palisades, New York, to Manhattan and back, crossing the George Washington Bridge and going along the Hudson River.

For a few years she had lived in Palisades with a woman named Doris Sanders. Originally from Indiana, Doris had come east to attend Columbia, and then during World War II worked as an economist for the Office of Price Administration. After the war, she was an advertising writer and a journalist. Together Pat and Doris wrote a picture book called *Miranda the Panda Is on the Veranda,* which Pat illustrated in black-and-white sketches. It was a silly book ("Mabel Grable, a sable, reads a fable at the table in the stable near the gable with a cable"). It was inspired by the books of Polly Cameron, who had already published *The Cat Who Thought He Was a Tiger* and *The Dog Who Grew Too Much.*

Pat's dedication was to M. C. H.—her mother, Mary Coates Highsmith.

Pat and Doris had rented a little barn in the woods near Sneden's Landing where they both had friends. When Pat and Doris broke up, Polly Cameron moved to the barn from New York.

When I came to know Polly, she told me she had been in love with Doris when Doris was living with Pat. She was invited to the barn one weekend. She wanted to do everything right.

Pat and Doris slept up in the loft, and Polly slept down on the couch in their small living room. She awakened early on a Saturday morning to see a snail on the floor near her shoes.

She was repelled by snails. She didn't ever imagine herself picking one up, but she didn't want it to be there when Pat and Doris came down for breakfast. She braced herself and got a paper towel from the kitchen. Out the door it went.

"Where's my snail, I wonder," Pat said when she came downstairs. "Have you seen a little snail, Polly?"

All weekend Polly lied that she knew nothing about a snail, and Pat searched for the creature in vain. Of course, the snail had been Pat's pet.

In *Deep Water*, 1957, Vic Van Allen, the murdering hero, raised snails in an aquarium in his garage, and in a later book one of Pat's short stories was called "The Snail Watcher."

Four

Those late April days Pat invited her friends to meet me, and she cooked for five or six guests at a time in her small kitchen. We also had my two close friends Tom Baird and Martha Wolfenstein to dinner. Pat claimed she was a "peasant cook." I would make her a "cooking drink" (she had "dressing drinks," "argument drinks," "sleepless night drinks," on and on). Without ever looking at a recipe she would make bouillabaisse, cassoulet, stew, or curry.

I liked most of her friends, especially one in particular: an art critic named Rosalind Constable. She was one of those lesbians who had a lifetime arrangement with a woman who lived elsewhere, similar to the kind the writer Janet Flanner had with Natalia Murray. If they couldn't always live in the same place because of work, if they couldn't always be true to one another because of passion, it was understood they would be together in their old age. Rosalind's partner lived in Santa Fe.

Rosalind was born in Britain, worked first for *Fortune* magazine, then became the cultural critic for *Time* magazine, as well as an art collector. She was witty, smart, and a good writer.

Another of Pat's favorites was an artist called Lil Picard, who could never come to dinner. Although she did not live with her husband, she ate dinner with him every night. It was a condition of whatever their arrangement was.

Finally Lil agreed to come just for dessert and coffee. She was a small, dramatic type, a shawl flung about her narrow shoulders, great Italian lace-ups beneath the hem of her Indian wraparound skirt. She wore lots of eye shadow, lipstick, and bright red nail polish.

Exotic and amusing, she was also bossy and proprietary. Upon arrival she was busy ordering Pat about ("Darling, find the terrible draft that's making me shiver!") but finally she settled down and began discussing Pat's mother.

This was not a favorite topic with Pat. In those years she was very attached to her mother, but Mrs. Highsmith was difficult. She, too, was bossy and possessive, and she had once made the mistake of telling Pat, in a joking manner, that probably the reason Pat loved the smell of turpentine was that she had swallowed some in an attempt to abort her.

Pat never forgot it.

Lil immediately asked me if I knew about the turpentine, and then told me while Pat squirmed. Lil was an artist of sorts who'd make peculiar collages (assorted lipsticks hanging from a comb) and always had gossip about the Cedar Bar crowd: Jackson Pollock, de Kooning, and others she knew only by sight.

Apparently, there was considerable rivalry between Mrs. Highsmith and Lil, or "Lily" as Mrs. H. called her in a letter she wrote me:

> Don't know if you have met Lily Picard or not. She is a Jewess from Germany and was just in time out of Germany with Hitler hot on her heels. Her husband also Jewish runs an antique shop on East 57th and deals mainly in fine furniture. They were also entertained at our Hastings home for dinner, and they spent the night. I had a local couple (neighbors) in to meet them.

The neighbors didn't like them. I found out after they arrived in this country they gambled their all in Wall Street and lost their shirts. He had it tough for a few years, but now he is doing better. She paints and has lovers on the side. At the time she had one named Stewart. She asked Pat (now tie this) if she could come up to my house for the weekend and bring Stewart.

Pat screamed "NO, NO, NO." So you see Pat knows more than she pretends, that outraged her. Well, later Lily had to have a major operation. Did Stewart pay for it? Certainly not. He left her cold. Pat furnished the money for the operation.

Years later with nothing ever said by Lily about paying her any part of it, Pat broached the subject and asked Lily if she thought she could start paying on the debt. Lily bawled her out and called Pat a stingy little sh— and a few other insults, and Pat took it.

Lily now has another lover tho she continues living with her husband and Pat says he knows it.

In the meantime, Lily came up to our house with Pat alone. She walked in the door where my husband was working with an assistant (an old friend of the family) and said, "Ooh, how intereesting, vis all zee art work."

I introduced them and Stanley soon excused himself and went down to mix drinks. She followed him down and sat on the top step leading down into our kitchen (3 steps down from a stair landing). He said she had exposed herself. He turned slightly and continued mixing and when he turned around she was really letting him have it.

It is amusing to have a guest in your house who is bent on making your husband. Since she lost all their

money she would say to me (and my home was not lav-
ishly furnished) "Vy do you need zees and zees and zees?"
And I, realizing her accent was phony said, "Because I
want zees, I imagine."

I did have a Steinway and a few antiques in fur-
niture I was particularly proud of. And oh, yes, I had a
Filipino house boy who literally dropped in my lap, and
that seems to make a terrific impression on her.

I was illustrating children's books and had a big
house and he fitted in beautifully in fixing breakfast,
and dinner, serving it in courses by candlelight. He once
was house boy and butler to Leeds, the tin people and
was on their yacht in the Caribbean and in Palm Beach
and knew of no other way of serving. All our friends
thought we were in the money when they saw him for
the first time.

He was small, slight, attractive and graceful as a
ballet dancer, and Lily was attracted to him, too....
I asked Pat how did she have a lover and continue
living with her husband? Pat said she and her husband
had a purely platonic relationship and that she couldn't
stand his approach. Nice set-up?

All this Pat accepts. She says she admires Lily
because she works so hard at art and was going places.
I insist she is going nowhere as she is a complete phony
and no phony can succeed at art.

And now we come to—

This long letter from Mrs. Highsmith was a complaint
about all the women Pat was attached to—some lovers,
others just friends.

She had this to say about Rosalind Constable:

One day on a Fifth Avenue bus with Pat, she said, "Oh, Mother, there's Rosalind." Our bus had stopped for a light and R. was crossing and I got a GOOD look.... I disliked her on sight.

In a short story of Pat's, called "Under a Dark Angel's Eye," published years later, the main character remembers his mother's "unremitting dislike and criticism of every girl he had ever brought to the house."

Pat loved entertaining. She was a gracious host, and the gin, scotch, and wine flowed.

She was very unselfconscious about showing me affection in front of her friends. I liked that about her. She would hold my hand at the table or, passing by, rub my neck, lean over, and say, "All right?"

I didn't love it when we were in the aisle of a supermarket or walking along the street. She would grab my hand and swing it, or put her arm around me in a store.

I couldn't seem to get past my small-town, WASP upbringing, and I told myself I'd probably be as uncomfortable if it was a male doing it. But that wasn't the truth. In the '50s it was hard for most of us to be openly gay.

Pat would say, "The only difference between us and heterosexuals is what we do in bed. It's nobody's business what goes on in the bedroom."

"But we don't spend our lives horizontally. We have the same kind of lives they do, without acceptance."

"I don't care for acceptance," from Pat.

That kind of conversation would launch one of my diatribes about how different we were from any other minority group. Unlike blacks, Jews, and others who faced discrimination, we grew up without a peer group. We had no support from our families, either. The church saw us as sinners and the law saw us as illegal.

"And how about all the lies we tell our parents?" I finished one of my speeches once. "We tell lies, and we write lies home. How about all that?"

"I never do and I never did," Pat said flatly.

"You never lied to your mother and father?"

"My mother and my *stepfather*. I never brought it up. I *tried* to like men. I like most men better than I like women, but not in bed."

"Do your mother and stepfather know you're gay?"

"I think they assume I am," Pat said.

Before Kit moved back to her apartment on Horatio Street, she met Pat one evening.

"She stood up when I came in the room," she told me, "and when we moved out to the kitchen she stood back and gave a little bow and signaled with her hand for me to go ahead. You've got yourself a real gentleman, M. J."

Five

The Grapevine, a trendy lesbian bar, had a raunchy quality to it. On weekends and some busy weeknights, a bouncer took five dollars admission, stamped your wrist with a purple mark, and gave you two drink tickets. It was not in Greenwich Village, either, but in the east 30s. Still, it was very popular because it was run by Gwen Saunders and Mia Fabrizzio, veteran barkeeps in the lesbian world. Their names always drew the more affluent and sophisticated women, along with the younger wannabes.

I went there one night with a good friend and would-be writer, Meg Terry. She was eager to meet Highsmith, who would join us later. This was before Meg's plays were receiving notice in the *Sunday New York Times* theater section, before they were being performed off-Broadway at La Mama, and before she'd written the first anti-Vietnam War play, *Viet Rock*.

Pat was having dinner that night with her old photographer-friend, Rolf Tietgens.

When I told Mia that Pat Highsmith would join us later, she led us to the back room, more private than the bar.

"I *heard* you were seeing Pat Highsmith," she told me, and then she sat down, as she always did when she was ready to give and receive gossip.

"Do you know the story behind her trip to Mexico?" she asked.

Mia had dark hair and green eyes, and she looked a bit like a young Patricia Neal.

"What story?" I said.

"She went to Mexico with Mary Ronin."

"And Ronnie?"

"No Ronnie," Mia said firmly.

I knew about Mary and Ronnie, the way lesbians and gay men in New York City often knew about others without ever having met them. Gay gossip flourished the way gossip does in any clan or colony. Names were dropped of this movie star and that television producer who were "guests at the party," code for gay. We thrived on borrowed glory, all of us closeted, many from families in small towns, suddenly in a world where we needed police protection to have drinks in bars catering to us. We took some small comfort in proclaiming that Noël Coward was one of us, W. H. Auden was, Katherine Cornell, Eva Le Gallienne, James Baldwin, Rudolf Nureyev, E. M. Forster, Mary Renault, on and on.

Manhattan gays had their own "celebrities," too—ones who were more affluent, successful, or glamorous, usually a few years older. Ronnie Bamburger and Mary Ronin were minor celebrities to those of us just beginning to find our way around the gay world and New York. Ronnie was a rich, uptown lesbian, her money spouting from oil wells in the West.

Ronnie and Mary Ronin were a longtime lesbian couple, with a townhouse in the East 70s.

"Pat didn't go to Mexico with anyone," I said, and quickly added, "I don't *think*."

But I knew that Mia had all the dirt.

Most lesbian gossip was usually right on the mark, too. There was always more of it than there was gossip about gay men, because Manhattan gay men didn't live together or stay together that much. In those days it was very hard for a businessman to have a male roommate. You seldom heard of breakups between men, or men moving in with each other, or one man moving out. Gay men who *were* in long relationships seemed to be able to tolerate each other's unfaithfulness, as well. Often there was an understanding: Do what you want but don't soil the nest. The nest could be two apartments in the same building, or a summer home at Fire Island—whatever was considered the security blanket of being a couple.

"Now Pat wants to get back to Europe, I hear," Mia continued, "because her heart is broken. Mary won't leave Ronnie."

"Thanks for spoiling my evening," I said.

"Oh, honeys," she said (it was always "honey" with an *s*), "better to know now before you get that involved."

"I'm already that involved." I was thinking at least I finished my book. I'd been working hard, making up for the hangover days in the very beginning with Pat. At last we had some sort of schedule: dinner most nights, and she'd stay over at my apartment. Always she got up around seven and left. Like me, in the best of times, Pat worked five days a week.

Mia said, "Honeys, be realistic. This woman isn't Kit. She isn't going to take care of you. Writers need wives! She's not wife material."

"Pat probably needs a wife, too," Meg spoke up.

"I know that! That's why this would never work," said Mia. Then she laughed and drawled, "Besides, I want Pat Highsmith for myself."

But she could not get me to laugh it off. I knew there had to be some truth to it.

"So what?" Meg said. "You were actually *living* with someone when you met Pat."

"But I'm not still in love with Kit," I said. I was already rationalizing everything I'd been doing with the old psychosemantic bull: I love Kit but I'm not *in* love with Kit. That could be twisted to "I loved you but I never liked you," or "You liked me but you never loved me," on and on. Good for a drunken heart-to-heart analysis of what went wrong, when what went wrong was that there was someone new.

"Are you going to believe Mia Fabrizzio?" Meg asked me.

"She usually knows what's going on."

"M. J., she makes things more than they are."

"But why is Pat running off to Europe when she just got home? That's definitely suspicious."

Meg laughed. "Remember *Othello*. '*Trifles light as air / Are to the jealous confirmations strong / As proofs of holy writ.*'"

I bought us another round.

By the time Pat arrived, ushered in grandly by Mia, Meg and I were high. Meg shook hands with Pat, and then she ran out of the Grapevine to hail a cab back to her apartment.

"What have you two been up to that you got so drunk?" Pat asked.

"It's what *you've* been up to that made *me* high!"

Pat listened while I berated her for never telling me a thing about Mary.

"Why should I have?" she said. "It's over."

"Then why are you running off to Europe?"

"I told you. I can't work well here."

"What if she'd said she'd leave Ronnie?"

Pat shook her head. "She never would. Ronnie's too rich."

Pat stood up without finishing her drink and I got scared. I think I was scared I'd lose her just as easily as I'd met her. I said, "Are you coming home with me?"

"Can we drop the subject of Mary?"

"Yes. I won't mention it again."

And I was true to my word, for a long time, but there was no one, probably not even one of Pat's or my own bent fictional characters, who became more obsessed. I remember James Sandoe, the mystery reviewer for the *Herald Tribune*, commenting that Vin Packer (my suspense pseudonym) had a good understanding of "the dislodged mind."

I phoned everybody for information about Mary Ronin, and I even took the bus up to the 70s, to walk past the townhouse, just off Fifth Avenue. I couldn't help thinking about Pat going to New Jersey to see where the customer lived who would later inspire *The Price of Salt*.

It was a Saturday, and, by one of those strange coincidences writers of fiction can never use as plot material, there was Mary, on the doorstep, polishing the brass mail slot. She was of medium height, stocky, blondish gray hair, with a pretty Irish face, somewhere in her fifties. She had on jeans and an old navy sweater, a bandanna holding her hair back.

I crossed the street, even though I knew she didn't know me.

What I'd found out about her was that she was an artist, that she had a job with an advertising agency drawing cars, that she was supposed to be a superb cook, and that she had been with Ronnie about ten years. In those days, that was a long track record for a lesbian relationship.

Although Pat had claimed that Mary stayed in the relationship because of Ronnie's money, all my sources told me Mary made a good advertising salary. It was something entirely different, I was told. It was a home Mary wanted, a home life. She was afraid Pat was too much of a wanderer, and too eager to make her life in Europe.

Six

"This is the worst I've ever seen you," my friend, Tom Baird, said. "You are besotted by that woman!"

Tom worked at the Frick Collection on Fifth Avenue. We'd met when he moved across the hall from me on East 94th Street. Our apartments were the only ones on the fourth floor, and we had wonderful times together, cooking dinner every night, having nightcaps when we came home from our dates, and just "hanging out." After I met Kit, I moved to Greenwich Village. Sometimes I'd meet him, as I did that day, for lunch at the Metropolitan Museum of Art. He began enumerating all the changes in my life since I met Pat.

I had begun refusing party invitations, fearing Pat would meet someone at one of them. Fortunately, when she was with someone, she wasn't that fond of bars. We cooked in a lot, read together in the same room, and listened to music while she sketched my cats, or, if we were at her apartment, the stolid, black Spider, who didn't like to play, didn't react to catnip, mostly just sat watching Pat. I began to read into his steady staring at her: It was a look of longing, I decided, as though he knew she could take off on that tramp steamer any day.

Several times Pat spoke of going to Marseille, and always she would say, "Come along. Would you? We could get an apartment. Just try it for a year or two."

"We hardly know each other," I'd tell her. But I was thinking about it, never mind Kit, whom I still loved, never mind my valued professional apartment on West 13th Street which I waited so long to get, my five cats, and the gay friends I had found in New York City, who were like family to me. Never mind Tom, Tom complained. We never saw much of each other in those days.

I asked Tom what he thought about my getting an advance from Gold Medal Books and going to Europe to live awhile. I'd never taken advances. My habit was to write the book, then receive payment.

"Go to Europe to live with *Pat?*" Tom asked and didn't wait for my answer. "I hope not! You'd be too much in her shadow. You don't need that right now. You need to get published in hardcover, to build your savings so you can afford to take time off, instead of taking an advance from Gold Medal."

Tom argued that this was not the right time, and she was not the right person.

"I thought you liked her."

"I do. I particularly like speaking German with her. She has the most remarkable accent for someone who taught herself."

"But?"

"She's too much the featured player, M. J. Write that book about famous suicides you've always talked about. It'll be taken by a hardcover house. *Then* go. She'll wait for you if she's worth anything, or she'll come back to be with you."

Pat had no idea how conflicted I was where she was concerned: that I was so jealous, that I had consulted with Tom about the possibility of going to Marseille with her, that I had even toyed with the idea of writing her after she left for Europe and telling her it was all over.

I wasn't sure I could continue in an affair with someone I was so smitten with. I was always on guard: afraid a potential rival would catch her eye, afraid Mary would leave Ronnie for Pat—the whole, horrible gamut.

I began trying to distract myself from the thought of her leaving, oddly enough with notes on that book about suicide. Ever since Tom and I had met each other I'd talked about wanting to write it. Having Pat suddenly in my life made me want to be something more than a paperback writer. I vowed that as soon as I finished *The Girl on the Bestseller List*, I would try a few chapters and an outline, and see if I could interest an agent or a hardcover editor. I wanted to feature a major figure in his or her profession: perhaps James Forrestal, former Secretary of Defense, who had jumped to his death; Hart Crane, poet, who had thrown himself off a ship; and Virginia Woolf, writer, who had also drowned herself.

Wilhelm Stekel was my choice as the psychiatrist/psychoanalyst. There was a very high suicide rate among them, although dentists were at the top of the list. Artists were up there, too. I wanted to write about Nicholas de Stael, a painter whom a friend of mine collected, but there was not enough information about him in English. I chose Arshile Gorky instead.

Helping me think this through with discussions about suicide was my good friend Martha Wolfenstein, a Manhattan child psychoanalyst. We'd become friends after I took a course she taught at The New School. Since her husband worked in France, she had free time, and we discovered that we both loved going to movies and having dinner after.

Sixteen years older than I was, Martha became a major influence on me. I even fell into a strange speech pattern she had, her voice rising on certain words and stressing them. "Anna *Freud* was there *of* course." Pat teased me about it and called me The Mimic. She said the suicide book was my way of becoming an analyst like Martha.

As I began making notes about Gorky, Martha introduced me to Ethel Schwabacher, who had been a protégée of his. She was also a devoted Freudian who claimed Gorky might have been saved, never mind that he had cancer, had lost his paintings in a fire, and was being deserted by his wife. If only he had been able to keep the appointment she had arranged for him with a leading analyst, he might still be alive. Martha nodded in agreement.

I was beginning to become my old self, I believed, and even Pat commented on how much happier I'd seemed than when she first met me. Some of that unhappiness was the split between Kit and me, but more was the high/low passion Pat provoked. One minute pure elation, the next certainty that there was someone else in the picture...or that there would be, once she was out of my sight.

I decided to call my suicide book *Sudden Endings*. I agreed with Tom that at this point in my life I should put my energy into my career.

Tom was about to take his own advice, for he had accepted a job in Washington, D.C., at the National Gallery. By the time he got up the courage to tell me, he had already located a townhouse he was purchasing in Georgetown; he was a month away from leaving.

"But you moved away first," he teased, "for Kit."

Seven

One Saturday night Pat was going to take me to Café Nicholson, on East 58th Street, for dinner. She said there was a parrot there who said, "Birds don't talk."

I decided that at dinner I'd tell her about Lilo, the first gay woman I'd met in New York. She worked at a very commercial/touristy gay nightclub on Second Avenue, called the 181. Most of the waiters (except for Lilo) were major butches, who dressed as men even away from the club. All of the entertainers were male transvestites who appeared in ball gowns singing, "Balls, balls, how I love balls." I'd gone there with an old college boyfriend, trying to find a gay bar when I first came to New York. A cab driver had recommended it.

The customers, of course, were all out-of-towners thinking they'd found the secret homosexual life.

The minute I saw Lilo, I fell for her. She had black hair and blue eyes, a poodle called Maggie, suede coats, silk shirts and pants, and always the scent of Celui clung to her. Her mother ran a famous New York restaurant, and Lilo was the rebel in the family. She was amused by my "crush" and she let me hang around her and her friends, at her apartment on Charles Street, across from Seville. This was a serious, role-playing crowd: butch/femme. Lilo said I was a "ki ki," the slang for someone in-between.

Lilo had a parrot named Parrot Como, after the singer Perry Como. Shortly after the bird flew out the window, Lilo, a lesbian for ten years, fell in love with a man. She marked the metamorphosis by the bird's flight.

I loved telling Pat stories, and hearing those she told me. It was one of the pluses of our relationship. We liked to listen to each other. We saved our good stories for special times.

"Nicholson's has a wonderful wine list," she said, "and we've never been uptown together. We'll dress up and celebrate our two-month anniversary."

That afternoon I called Kit to come over and help me choose what to wear. We'd stayed good friends. That seemed indigenous to gay life—your best friends were your former lovers.

Even though Kit made a mock exasperated face, she picked out a silk suit she'd bought me years ago at Saks.

We were looking over my heels and handbags, giggling, having fun, when the phone rang. Pat's ship had come in. A tramp steamer sailing near midnight had a cabin for her.

"I have to be there by nine," she said.

"Okay. Fine." I was devastated.

She said, "I know it isn't."

"Well, there's nothing you can do."

"I have to get my typewriter from the repair shop, and pack. It's almost six now."

"Let's not see each other," I said. "It's too sad."

"I wanted to show you Café Nicholson so badly."

"Never mind. Kit's here. We'll go to the Village Green. A lot of friends are going there tonight."

"Oh, love, I hate this."

"So do I."

"I'll write you a lot. A lot!"

"Okay." But she wasn't saying I *have* to see you before I go.

"And I love you a lot," she said.

"So do I love you, but I can't talk anymore. Please."

We said good-bye, and after I hung up I began to cry. I almost never cried except at happy endings of corny movies.

"I'm through with her now," I said when I could get a grip.

"I can see that," said Kit wryly.

"No, I'm going to write her that it's over. I can't put up with this. It's too hurtful. She'll never stay with me."

Kit calmed me down and talked me into doing what I'd told Pat we were going to do.

We'd have dinner at the Village Green. It was an old Greenwich Village restaurant, newly soliciting a gay clientele. Restaurateurs sometimes sought a gay dinner crowd who would stay on to drink, and attract late-night drinkers, as well. They would hire a popular gay piano man. Sometimes these places caught on, but mostly they didn't last because the police would pressure them for payoffs.

Kit knew the new pianist there, Charles DeForrest. "I told him your discovery during your suicide research: that no famous musicians or sports stars ever killed themselves. He's fascinated."

"I bet he is," I muttered, but I appreciated Kit's attempt to help me get past something by talking about my work, and staying near me. She was always a calming influence, even under this circumstance: helping me recover from her rival's departure. When we'd lived together, she'd burned orange peels to give our kitchen a pleasant scent, and taken Kelly, our crabby old Siamese cat, for a walk down the hall on her shoulder, telling Kelly she knew Kelly had to get away from the others for a bit.

It was crowded at the Village Green. We got a table not too near the piano. The specialty was my favorite: prime rib. Baked potato. Fresh chopped spinach. Good red wine. The old days of horizontal food, American food, unlike now with the scallops on top of the mashed potatoes, the red pepper strips on top of the scallops, salsa sauce poured over everything: a vertical nightmare.

Charles knew all the oldies: "I Remember You," "Lush Life," "I've Got It Bad and That Ain't Good."

Friends were there. It was one of those nights that the next day you'd say "*Everyone* was there!"

Then suddenly Pat was, too.

Her duffel bag was over her shoulder, and she was carrying her portable typewriter. She was standing in the doorway of the room looking for me. Next thing I knew she was behind me, leaning down to tell me over the noise, "I couldn't leave you."

Eight

That August night was a scorcher. I met Pat's return flight at LaGuardia Airport. She had gone to Texas for a family visit. She deplaned, looking glum, raising her hand in a salute, brushing her long hair back, once on each side in a familiar gesture. She wanted a drink immediately, also familiar.

"Did something bad happen?" I asked.

"No. It was the usual."

We sat for an hour in the lounge at the airport while she talked about her mother.

"It's not my fault she never became the famous artist she wanted to be," she grumbled.

"Did she say it was your fault?"

"She doesn't have to. I know that's what she thinks."

Pat had written me from Fort Worth:

August 13. 59

Last evening, my uncle Claude and aunt by marriage Norene again. The Student Prince, excellent background for daydreaming and thinking about the book I am writing. P. 166 at present, should be 174 by the end of today. I accepted my uncle's invitation for a nightcap chez lui, and from them heard worse news of my mother. She wrote a suicide note last Feb. or March and told a close friend of hers that she tore it up. I do not know (neither does my uncle) whether my stepfather knows of this or not, and I don't think I'll burden him

further by telling him of it.... I shall now work on
getting my mother to have at least one session with a
psychologist, as this thing ought to be diagnosed and
labeled, if possible. I meant to say psychiatrist. Every
proposal of activity she politely declines, though
according to my aunt she will come along if more or less
ordered to do so, as a child is told what to do....

I am expecting a letter from you tomorrow. Please.
Much love and wishing you a good state of mind
—the writer's tool—no filthy pun, my dear. Pat.

I asked Pat, "What did your mother say when you broached the subject of her seeing a psychiatrist?"

"That she didn't need one. That what she needed was some respect from me."

"Uh-oh."

I sympathized with Pat because my relationship with my own mother had been deteriorating ever since I'd told her that I was a lesbian. She never stopped mentioning how she wanted grandchildren, or as she once put it how I'd "missed the boat." ("What boat is that, Mother?" "The boat my grandkids would be on.") I think Pat's mother wasn't easy with Pat's homosexuality, either. She wanted Pat.

There was a time when the feeling was mutual. Pat never denied how attached she was to her for most of her young life, how she wanted so badly to please her and never could. She would complain that her mother's criticism depressed her terribly.

Pat always drove my British Ford convertible at night, because I didn't like to drive after dark. We put the top down when we left the airport, and Pat held my hand most of the way back to Manhattan.

"Can we go away from New York, somewhere we can be alone?" Pat asked.

"Fire Island?" My friend Martha Wolfenstein had grown attached to Fair Harbor, ever since she and her husband had shared a cottage there one summer with Kit and me.

"I'm not in a mood for Martha and Nathan," Pat said. "They're too heavy, even for a few hours."

I told Pat that Martha had said their cottage was empty during the week, and she wished someone would make use of it.

"Then let's go!" Pat was suddenly all smiles. "Let's go tomorrow!"

Spider, Pat's serious black cat, had been temporarily integrated into my household, so we did not have to stop at her apartment that night. Pat would put my car in the garage next door, but first she pulled up in front of 117 West 13th. There was a cat in every one of my apartment's six ground floor windows.

Pat handed me a small gift-wrapped box, saying I couldn't open it until she'd put the car away.

I took her bag and waited inside for her, four Siamese and one Persian rushing to greet me. Not Spider, however. He still sat in the window looking out, as though he knew Pat would appear.

When she came through the door, he sauntered past my cats and waited for her to pick him up and hold him against her shoulder. Only then did he purr. He hadn't purred since she'd been gone.

"Can I open my present?" I asked.

While I unwrapped it she said she'd found it in a jewelry store in Fort Worth. What she liked about it was that something had been engraved inside the ring, then rubbed away, all except *rememb.*

It was an old gold wedding band that Pat put on my third finger, right hand.

"Will you always wear it?"

I said yes, I would.

There were blissful days ahead at Fair Harbor: making love, sunbathing, reading, walking along the shore, cooking dinner for each other, and lingering into the night having drinks and listening to music.

For once, I could talk unselfconsciously about writing. With other women I'd often felt it was egotistical to spout off story ideas, or maybe just boring for them. But Pat enjoyed talking shop, although like me she did not discuss ongoing work.

I told her I'd always wanted to edit an anthology of lesbian and homosexual material, as Ann Aldrich. The Aldrich books I wrote were very successful paperbacks, going into two and three printings of 400,000 each. I needed money while I researched my suicide book.

I explained to Pat that in the anthology I wanted to include things like Freud's essay "A Case of Homosexuality in a Woman," Simone de Beauvoir's "The Lesbian" from *The Second Sex*, fiction like de Maupassant's "Paul's Mistress," …and "how about the last chapter of *The Price of Salt?*"

"I'd be in good company," she said.

Then I tried out an idea on her that had come to me when she was in Texas.

I quoted that part of Pat's last chapter in *Salt,* when Therese is thinking that it was Carol and only Carol she loved...that "it would be Carol in a thousand cities, in a thousand houses..." etcetera.

I asked Pat, "What do you think of the title *Carol, in a Thousand Cities?*"

"It's a good title. It's better than *The Price of Salt.* I wish I'd thought of it."

"You did," I said.

Every time we talked about our writing, I felt closer to her. She told me that she, too, had felt "egomaniacal" talking book ideas to other lovers.

"We make a good team," Pat said, "and I'm glad we have this summer."

In a conversation I had with Pat's mother, before Pat and I left for Fire Island, she'd said, "I can't believe Pat's giving up her plan to go to Europe."

I'd answered the phone in Pat's apartment, as she'd told me to while she was taking Spider to the vet.

I knew Mary Highsmith was fishing. I said something about work Pat had to do and she cut me off, saying her novel was finished, even the copyediting was. It was one of those times I wished I could just say, "We've fallen in love." Instead I mumbled something about Pat's wanting to relax at the ocean, that a cottage was loaned to us on Fire Island.

She fished some more. "I suppose you're going to Fire Island to hang out with that Janet Flanner and her girlfriend."

I pretended to Mrs. Highsmith we hadn't made plans to see them.

"You'll see them," she said adamantly. "Pat can't resist them!"

In fact, they were the only people Pat said we "must see" while we were on the island. They had a cottage a few miles away, at Cherry Grove.

For homosexuals in the '50s, Cherry Grove and Fire Island Pines were Nirvana. This was particularly true for males. There were Manhattan businessmen who would have a Fire Island outfit in their offices, for changing into late Friday afternoons, before they caught the train to Sayville, Long Island. The pants were a little tighter, the shirts and cashmere sweaters in ice cream colors. The ferries leaving from Sayville went to the Pines and the Grove.

Cherry Grove was notorious as a homosexual community, its name beginning to creep into popular comedians' jokes. There was even a postcard showing a very nelly man wearing a huge picture hat, lying prone on the sand, with the caption "Mother thinks I'm at Ocean Beach." Ocean Beach, a few miles away, was the oldest and most populated community on Fire Island, a straight vacation spot for singles and young marrieds.

It was often the male homosexual who searched for and found the beautiful, little-known communities like Provincetown, Fire Island, the Hamptons, places that ultimately caught on with the majority. Before the hoi polloi arrived, they could dress as they pleased, dance together, cruise and camp and flaunt their partners and lovers and friends.

But lesbians, too, could walk the walk and talk the talk there.

The first time I visited Fire Island, I went to Cherry Grove with Tom and Kit and some psychiatrist friends of Tom. That was in 1953. We all paid $50 to stay for the weekend in a small cottage.

At dinner in Duffy's Hotel, I realized I hadn't brought my wallet. I was worried about the money I'd left behind. I didn't want anyone to interrupt their dessert and coffee, so I walked back to the cottage alone, using a flashlight to see.

It was a dark night with only a hazy moon overhead, periodically hidden by clouds. Suddenly, I heard thumping steps coming toward me, and I saw the outline of an enormous man. There was no way to escape him. It was quite a jump down on both sides of the narrow boardwalk, and I would not make much progress running through the brambles. I was trapped. My heart began to pound as he came closer. He had a flashlight, too, and it was suddenly aimed at his penis, which was large and erect. Then he put the flashlight on my face.

Before I said anything, he blurted out, "Oh, migod, I'm sor-ry! I am sor-ry. I did not *dream* you were a female!" He had a Jamaican accent, this huge black man, and he kept apologizing.

"It's okay," I said.

"All is well that will end well," he called out after me.

That was one of the lovely things about that part of the island: There was no menace for females alone at night.

Nine

Janet Flanner was famous for her "Letter from Paris" columns in the *New Yorker*, under the pseudonym Genêt. Natalia Murray represented the Italian book company, Rizzoli.

Our dinner invitation had come when Pat and Janet ran into each other in New York, and Pat mentioned that we were going to be in Fair Harbor. A date was made then and there because there were no telephones in island cottages. Pat made a Friday night date. We planned to stay overnight with them, in the Grove. We would leave for New York on Saturday morning from Fair Harbor, before Martha and Nathan arrived.

Pat carried a large straw bag with a bottle of French wine, the picture book she'd written with Doris Saunders *(Miranda the Panda Is on the Veranda)*, our pajamas, sweaters, and cigarettes.

On the jeep ride there, Pat told me she'd done something really gauche to Janet once. She was traveling in Europe, and had sent ahead a trunk, since she was going to settle for a while in France. It had to be picked up in twenty-four hours in Paris. Pat would not be in Paris until two days after the trunk arrived. She called Janet and asked her to please arrange for the trunk to be picked up and delivered to Janet's apartment.

"I'll never know where I got the nerve," she said. "Janet even made it clear that it was a terrible imposition, that she had to go there herself, *in person*, but I kept insisting, like one of my psycho heroes. I hardly knew her then, too."

"Did she ever mention it after that time?"

"Never. But it's all I think of when I'm around her. How could I ever have been so nervy?… You'll see—she's rather formidable."

I liked her immediately. Janet, sixty-seven, looked like a Maine fisherman with her sunburned face and white hair, in old jeans and a crisp white shirt. Natalia, ten years younger, by far the femme and the boss, was bustling about making us drinks, getting dinner, in yellow slacks and blouse with a yellow apron.

Natalia had a writer son, Bill Murray, and a granddaughter named for her. She spoke French with Pat while she marinated meat she'd cook over the coals outside.

I stayed with Janet in the living room. Their cottage was on the bay side of the island.

"I hear you have talent," Janet began the conversation. "I hope that's true."

When she asked me if it was my first visit to the island, I boasted that I was there in the early '50s.

She said, "Natalia and I began coming here together in the forties…."

She was glancing through the picture book, which Pat had illustrated as well as written in collaboration with Doris Saunders, a stunning, slender brunette I had seen only once.

" 'A newt on a flute can toot,' " Janet quoted from the book, wincing. Then she turned to the dedication page. "Who's M. C. H.?" she asked me.

"Mary Coates Highsmith. Her mother."

"Ah! The mother."

I decided not to mention the fact that Pat's latest book, *This Sweet Sickness,* which I had yet to read at that point, was also dedicated simply "To my mother."

There were martinis before dinner, which I knew better than to drink. I had scotch on the rocks. There were several bottles of red wine for dinner: steak, baked potato, salad, and fresh string beans.

We talked about writing, and then a lot about the televised hearings Senator Joseph McCarthy had conducted, charging that a Communist spy ring was operating in the United States. That was back in 1954. To see them on television, Janet and Natalia had to go into New York, since there was no electricity anywhere on the island.

I told them that that very summer, I had been at Fair Harbor for a month, and living a few doors away from Leslie, a TV writer who had been blacklisted. A somewhat placid and unpolitical Price Waterhouse CPA had gladly lent his name to Leslie's teleplays, garnering praise from girls he dated for having this unsuspected, liberal passion.

Natalia quoted Lillian Hellman's assertion that she could not and would not "cut my conscience to fit this year's fashion."

Janet winced again; she was good at wincing.

It was a while before I noticed Pat wasn't joining in the conversation. I had observed this when we were with Martha and Nathan one night, but they were discussing psychoanalysis. That time I thought Pat didn't participate because she didn't quite approve of it. She had a disdain of the "being shrunk fad."

With Martha and Nathan she'd murmured sarcastically that she heard Freud had stopped all sexual relations when he was forty. (Nathan, with his mocking grin: "Oh, where did you *hear* that?")

Giggling over some unknown person's description of Hellman looking like the figurehead on a ship, Pat was finally joining the conversation. "Someone else said it, I didn't," said Pat. "I don't know where the quotation came from." No one thought the remark was as amusing as Pat thought it was. Blank expressions.

Then Janet snapped, "Oh, why are we talking about this Stalinist, anyway?"

That ended that.

"Why don't we buy you a nightcap at the Sea Shack before you head back?" Natalia said.

We were both flabbergasted. We did not meet each other's eyes, afraid to react and give away our mistaken notion we were to be overnight guests.

While our hosts did a minimal amount of cleaning up, Pat took me aside and whispered, "I'm sorry! We'll get a taxi back."

At the Sea Shack, I was congratulating myself for staying sober. But at the bar, where, for some unknown reason, Janet and I were discussing Robert Frost, she put her arm around my shoulder and said, "I see great signs of brilliance in you, periodically washed away by waves of whiskey."

We both laughed hard, and I realized she was feeling no pain herself, made plain when Natalia's requests for her to leave became sharper. Then, a simple order: "Right now!"

We thanked them as we said goodnight and they said come again.

It was very late. The bar was closing.

"How much money do you have?" Pat asked me.

"None. Just my Diners Club card. I bought Janet and me drinks."

"I don't even have a charge card. I have exactly four dimes."

"We can still call a taxi. When we reach Fair Harbor, I'll have him stop in front of the cottage. I have cash there."

It was a good idea, but the taxi had stopped running.

The bartender suggested we try the hotel.

The Cherry Grove Hotel was built on the site of Duffy's, the once famous hotel/saloon that had burned to the ground in 1956. Old-timers at the Grove believed that was when the Grove began to change. Too many heterosexual sightseers. Too many groupie renters.

At the hotel we were told that they did not even have an empty closet.

Pat refused go back to Janet's and Natalia's. She didn't want them to know she'd misunderstood the invitation. They would be asleep by then, anyway. I finally agreed with Pat that somehow we'd do without them.

Early that morning, we woke up down on the beach, in the rain.

It was five-thirty. We moved up under a house on stilts, and changed from our shirts to the damp sweaters inside Pat's straw bag. We were shivering, embracing, laughing together, even managing to sleep in each other's arms for a while more.

About seven-thirty we sneaked along the boardwalk down to the store, because we didn't want to chance a meeting with Janet or Natalia. We called the taxi, but the storm (now thunder and lightning) was making it impossible for the jeep to come along the beach. We were stuck until the weather changed.

Our clothes and hair soaked, we got something to eat at the hotel with my Diners Club card.

Pat kept blaming herself "for ever thinking they'd invited us to stay overnight. It's like the trunk thing in Paris!"

"They've been on the island for years. They must know when taxis run," I said. "They never mentioned the time to us."

"When they're out here, they live in their own little world. I was surprised they invited us, in the first place."

Then Pat looked at me.

"You don't think they didn't like something we said?"

"No, I don't. This is just a misunderstanding."

Miserable, we stayed there until the jeep could pick us up, near two that afternoon.

The waves were high and there was little shoreline, but the taxi got us back to Fair Harbor where we were surprised by Martha and Nathan. They'd arrived for an overnight stay, with two friends.

"We're all going to have dinner together!" Martha said gaily. "I've brought steaks, and Elena and Nicky brought some wonderful wine!"

Ten

Even if Pat hadn't been hung over and exhausted, the dinner conversation might have irritated her anyway. Nicolas and Elena Callas were art critics, who were both writing books about Hieronymus Bosch. That night, with Martha and Nathan joining in, they were discussing Bosch-like images in Goya's etchings, *Los Caprichos*.

All four were in their forties, all intense and assertive, none of them uncomfortable with the idea that Pat and I weren't joining in.

Nicky, black-haired, bespectacled, tall, thin, and talkative, would argue his points with Nathan, balding, bespectacled, tall, thin, and just as talkative. Nathan was by far the calmer. He didn't shout and gesture as Nicky did. Martha and Elena, handsome middle-aged women, were directing their comments to each other.

I had seen this group in action before. I had heard the story of how Nicky had worked for years on his book about Bosch, only to have Elena suddenly begin one of her own.

"They're too much for me," Pat grumbled as we walked down to Kismet for a beer, after dinner, glad to get away for a while. "What is this obsession certain art critics have with Freudian theory?"

"They're probably being analyzed."

"Did I hear right? Did I hear Nicky say that bullfighting was symbolic transvestitism?"

"I heard something like that."

"I saw the books Nathan brought with him, one in French, one in German. *Too* much!"

"Well, *you* read both languages."

"I can get along in both, but I don't read both the same weekend. One novel is by a Marcel Jouhandeau. And the German one is by Robert Musil. I've never heard of either of them!"

"Now you have," I said. "Aren't you glad we stayed?"

Nicky and Elena Callas were going by jeep to Ocean Beach that night, to visit another couple. Martha and Nathan were leaving the very next afternoon, another reason they had insisted we stay. We could have the cottage to ourselves all week.

Kismet was in the opposite direction, about a half mile's walk from Fair Harbor. The lighthouse was nearby, and sometimes there were Coast Guard men in the small bar, but that Saturday night it was all but empty.

Over beers plus gin on the rocks for Pat, she told me she believed that psychoanalysis messed with your mind. She said she had read enough of Karl Menninger to know it was not for her.

When I pointed out that Menninger was a psychiatrist and not a psychoanalyst, we went on to have our first fight. Pat suggested that I was too in awe of "those people." She said she was about to create a character who copied the speech pattern of a psychoanalyst she had met a few times, and then began to take patients herself.

"Did you know you can be an analyst just by saying you're one?" she asked.

"I suppose you can be a lot of things just by saying you are," but I was getting angry, knowing she was angry at me, all because Martha and Nathan had talked us into dinner with the Callases.

I had no trouble connecting the dots: the character who copied the speech pattern, and ultimately became a phony analyst. And I remembered Pat chuckling about *Sudden Endings*, saying I was trying to be Martha.

"Martha's not even an M.D.," she said.

I let her have it then. I told her she was afraid of any discussion that went beyond small talk, that her idea of conversation was what was said at our lunch with José Garcia Villa and his boyfriend. I never knew when to stop in an argument. I went on to mention that she couldn't contribute anything at Janet's and Natalia's, on and on and on. Then I drunkenly conjectured that the reason she was so happy abroad was that there she had an excuse to be only superficially involved since she was still learning the languages.

We lumbered back to a darkened cottage. Our hosts were in bed.

When I woke up, I found Martha in the kitchen doing dishes, while Nathan and Pat conversed in French on the terrace.

"How do you like her?" I asked Martha.

She shrugged. "She's okay." So the feeling was mutual.

Pat claimed she never carried a grudge or remembered a fight. She probably didn't remember a fight in its totality, but she was good at injustice collecting. It was more like injustice cherishing.

Not that next morning, but again and again for a long time she would remind me that I said the reason she wanted to live abroad was to avoid in-depth conversation.

Still, it was refreshing to be with someone who seemingly simply skipped over a drunken argument of the night before...and upon seeing you, jumped up to greet you with a big smile, and to announce she'd squeezed a glass of orange juice for you and she'd get it from the kitchen.

Alone with Nathan, on the porch, I was suddenly the one who couldn't make conversation. I never knew what to say to Nathan. His most recent book was called *A Study of Bolshevism,* an extension of an earlier book titled *The Operational Code of the Politburo.* He and Martha had also written a book together: *Movies, A Psychoanalytic Interpretation.* He was working on a book about Soviet authority with their good friend Margaret Mead.

At one of their parties, a guest had remarked that Nathan was incapable of small talk.

I wanted Nathan to like Pat. This was their second meeting. He had met her very briefly when she'd picked me up after a dinner party at their apartment on Central Park West. That was the night of her remark about Freud's sex life.

I felt she had not been at her best that night or the night before with the Callases.

I finally said to Nathan, "Did you know Pat won France's Grand Prix de Literature Policière in 1957?"

"No, I didn't know that," Nathan replied. "But I like her anyway."

Our last night at the Fire Island cottage, Pat mentioned a conversation she'd had with Rosalind Constable, when she'd used the pay phone by the dock to cancel a dinner appointment they'd had.

She said, "Rosalind says Marcel Jouhandeau is a French highbrow." We were sitting on the deck after dinner, sipping Rémy Martin and listening to the ocean in front of us. The air was perfumed with the salty ocean smell and Gauloises.

We'd had a perfect five days together. I decided not to express surprise that Pat had bothered to discuss Jouhandeau while she was having to feed nickels and dimes into the phone box.

Pat continued, "You can ask Rosalind about any musician, writer, artist—she knows about all of them."

"Are you going to read Jouhandeau?"

"No. Rosalind said he's not my kind of writer."

For a while she sang Rosalind's praises, some sort of borrowed power to see her through another brush with Martha and Nathan, never mind that this one had only been overnight. They were the only friends I had who intimidated her.

She mentioned again that she didn't quite understand my devotion to Martha, even though she admitted Martha was smart—we were so "worlds apart."

I told Pat how much it meant to me to be friends with someone so formidable, who accepted my homosexuality. My college roommates had been horrified. I didn't even try discussing it with my parents, knowing their negative feelings on the subject. I couldn't afford psychoanalysis. There was absolutely no one to talk to about my life, no one to validate the decision I'd made to stop dating men…to be what I knew I was: a lesbian.

"Martha gave me confidence," I told Pat. "She still does. Both Martha and Nathan do. I figure that if I'm good enough to be friends with them, I'm doing all right."

"I can see what you mean," Pat said. "We carry around too much guilt. That's why I never make an announcement about it."

I laughed. "You don't have to. You hold girls' hands on the street, in the supermarket, in restaurants."

Pat was grinning. She tried a few times to get a lighter working in the wind, then gave up and lit a fresh cigarette from mine.

"Will you come with me?" she said.

"Where are you going?"

"If you won't come with me, will you write me every day?"

"What are you talking about?" I'd never known her to lose it when she was drinking, but for a minute I thought she had.

"I'm going to Europe September 21st," she said.

"Alone?"

"Since you won't come, yes. This time of year you need reservations…. I'll only be away for three or four months."

"This is a great way to tell me, while we're relaxing under the stars, on vacation."

"There's no great way to tell you," she said.

"You're right about that. I hate it!"

"Well, explode," she said. "Get it over with."

I looked at her and she looked back at me with this anxious expression, a frown across her forehead as though she anticipated the worst.

I had to laugh with affection, she sometimes seemed so vulnerable, and so prepared for the worst from those she loved. But I also felt dejected and *re*jected. I suddenly realized that the ring she'd brought back from Texas was a gesture of atonement.

I had never met anyone so drawn to Europe. I didn't understand that pull.

When Tom came from Washington for a visit, the next weekend, he said that *he* understood it. He used to go there every summer when he taught. "Be thankful it's not another woman." He shrugged and smiled ruefully. "It's just Paris, Rome, Florence, Venice."

Eleven

That fall, before Pat left, I was introduced to Ellen Hill, a past lover of hers, older, German, a small woman with a lot of style and opinions. Pat had a way of using backups in conversation when she recommended something or gave her view of anything. According to So-and-So, or So-and-So said, or So-and-So always.... Ellen Hill was a So-and-So, one of Pat's most referenced authorities.

We met at Pat's apartment on Irving Place for drinks before we went out.

It was a very warm September night. Ellen was wearing a cotton skirt and blouse with sandals. She complained that since Pat and I had chosen to wear pants, that limited our choice of a restaurant for dinner. I'd noticed that Pat was not wearing her usual man's white shirt and blazer. Probably in deference to Ellen, she had on a hand-embroidered man's Mexican wedding shirt she'd brought back from Oaxaca.

"Let's go to Fedora," I said. "It's usually okay."

By "okay" I meant they would not turn away women in pants, as some restaurants did even "downtown." Soho did not exist in those days, so downtown, for us, was Greenwich Village and the East Village. By "okay," I also meant that this restaurant was not too gay. I knew Ellen was the type who identified more with straights than gays, never mind her horizontal preferences. It was instantly obvious that outward appearances meant a great deal to Ellen. Although Fedora catered to many homosexual men, they were usually in suits with ties, and there were also straight people from the neighborhood.

"Where is this Fedora?" Ellen asked.

"Next to the place we had the arroz con pollo the other night," said Pat.

"Next to Seville?"

"Yes."

"Is it a homosexual restaurant?"

"Mostly," said Pat.

"Why should I be limited to a homosexual restaurant just because you two are homosexuals? The food usually isn't good in those places."

Pat shot her an exasperated look. "I didn't know you weren't homosexual, Ellen."

"You certainly didn't know I *was*," she answered. "I've always been mostly heterosexual."

"I'm sorry we're putting such limits on you," said Pat.

"Oh, well, we'll go where Marijane wants to go. I certainly don't want to get off on the wrong foot, insisting that we have a decent meal.... What's wrong with the Spanish place?"

The Spanish place was where we finally ate, bringing back memories of Lilo and her crowd, and Parrot Como flying out the window.

Pat, Ellen, and I shared a huge paella and a pitcher of sangria. Ellen kept reminding Pat that her poodle would welcome any chicken Pat had to spare.

When Pat went to the bathroom, Ellen confided that she was surprised Mary Ronin hadn't left the woman she was with, to be with Pat.

"Of course there's still time," she said.

I said sarcastically, "Thanks."

"I didn't mean that the way it sounded," Ellen said, "and I doubt that there *is* still time, even if Mary wants to be with Pat.... Pat's written her out of her system with her new book, *This Sweet Sickness*. That sums it up perfectly! Pat is a glutton for punishment!"

Foolishly, I was waiting for her to add something about Pat and me, something to acknowledge that we were a couple, as well, which would be another reason Pat wouldn't go back with Mary.

That didn't happen.

In fact, Ellen said, "You'll probably get tired of Pat and her wanderlust."

"I don't think so," I said.

"You hardly know her," she said.

For a few moments after Pat came back to the table, she and Ellen conversed in German.

I'd had enough drinks to complain to Pat later that I was tired of her speaking French or German, when the person we were with spoke English. Pat said that Ellen spoke in German because she was embarrassed that she hadn't brought any money with her, and could not split the bill with us. Pat had already told me numerous stories about Ellen's parsimonious nature. Pat herself had the same occasional inclination, but it was a habit born of necessity that most writers knew something about. Ellen, Pat often said, was just plain cheap.

"She wanted me to ask the waiter for some leftover chicken from the kitchen, too," Pat explained. "I forgot to save some for Klausie. When we were together, she always asked me to order something Klausie could eat for his dinner."

Pat seemed drawn to this kind of woman, the kind who expected things: from small gestures like holding doors open for them, to larger ones like living where and how *they* wanted to. Pat responded to these women by jumping up when they entered a room, grabbing the crease in her pants, then a little bow, ever the gentleman.

They were women who understood entitlement and who were baffled by a lover, male or female, who did not venerate them. There was also often a belittling side to them: Lil's mentioning how Mary Highsmith swallowed turpentine to abort Pat, the first night I met her, and Ellen's remarks about Mary and Pat, while Pat was in the restroom.

Before she left us (to go home and watch Edward R. Murrow's *Person to Person*) Ellen held out her hand and asked Pat for a quarter, to buy a loaf of bread. She wanted her morning toast.

When Pat put the quarter in her palm, Ellen said snidely, "How did I know you wouldn't give me one cent more!"

Then to me, "Good night, my dear. Good luck."

And she was off without even a nod in Pat's direction.

She made me determined to show Pat a more gentle and giving side of love, if only I could keep her.

That was the fatal difference: An Ellen thought Pat lucky to have her, while I bargained with the gods to make her stay in my life.

Twelve

"Mary Ronin?"

"Yes."

Then I would hang up.

Caller identification was not even on the drawing boards in those days, so I could make these anonymous calls. But this telephone game did not set to rest the notion that Pat was traveling with someone in Europe.

I envisioned her stopping off at American Express to pick up letters I'd write, while a lover waited back at a pensione or in a nearby café. I could not imagine someone who'd just fallen in love not only going ahead with a trip abroad, but also keeping to her plan to stay until February.

For months I didn't write her because of that. Not writing her did not mean not being involved with her. Now I use words like *smitten* and *besotted* to describe how I felt about her, but then I thought of it as the first time I was ever in love.

It was also the first time I ever paid to learn a foreign language. Pat's favorite—German. I enrolled at The New School.

It was the first time Tom had ever flown up from Washington specifically to see me on urgent business. That was to talk to me about this "scheme of yours" he said could end with me in prison. I was about to submit a change-of-address slip to the post office, for all first class mail to Mary Ronin, c/o my 13th Street address. Then, after sorting through her mail to see if there was a letter from Highsmith, I would use an ink stamp to eradicate my address and shove her forwarded letters down the gold mail slot at Ronnie Bamburger's townhouse. Of course, I would steam open and read any letters from Patricia Highsmith. I was sure there would be some. I wouldn't have been surprised if in one Pat mentioned where and when they would rendezvous. In Paris? In Rome? Eventually, of course, I planned to file another change-of-address restoring the first class mail to Mary.

"Someday you're going to look back and see that you were completely mad in this period of your life," Tom argued with me. "And it won't be at all amusing. Mail theft is a felony. You'll end up over in the Women's House of Detention, shouting down at Kit and me that you'd like us to buy you those Gauloises cigarettes you're smoking now!"

In those days the top floors of that women's jail, in Greenwich Village, was filled with prostitutes and hookers. We'd barely be able to see them in their cells, calling down to lovers and family gathered on Sixth Avenue that they needed Halo shampoo or a carton of Old Golds.

Tom finally convinced me not to fool with the U.S. Mail.

He said he hated Washington, that he was little more than an escort to old ladies from whom the museum hoped to receive funds or remembrances in wills.

"I wish we were back on 94th Street," he said. "And barring that I wish I was back at Princeton, writing. Not the long-awaited thesis, either. A novel!"

"I wish we were back on 94th, too."

The book I was working on was not a new Vin Packer, nor the suicide book. Instead, I was putting together the

Ann Aldrich anthology about lesbian life that I would call *Carol, in a Thousand Cities.... It would be Carol in a thousand cities, a thousand houses, in foreign lands where they would go together, in heaven and in hell.*

I was getting permissions from the Hogarth Press for Freud's essay "The Psychogenesis of a Case of Homosexuality in a Woman," from the publishers of Clara Thompson's "Changing Concepts of Homosexuality," and Simone de Beauvoir's "The Lesbian," on and on, ending with a chapter from *The Illusionist* by Françoise Mallet-Joris.

While friends told me about TV shows like *The Twilight Zone, The GE Theater,* and *Alfred Hitchcock Presents,* I, who was formerly mesmerized by the tube, announced I was planning to give away my TV set.

I also established a telephone friendship with Polly Cameron, who was living in the old barn Pat had rented with Doris, up in Palisades, New York. We thought we might write some kind of lightweight book together, our own little *Miranda the Panda,* with Polly illustrating.

I drove up to Palisades and visited Polly, as an excuse to talk all night about Pat. We got an idea for a book about a hangover. I doubted that we would ever follow through on it. I just wanted to hear about Pat from someone who was friends with her.

Pat knew none of this.

It was her habit to write loving messages across paper napkins from restaurants, hotels, and bars, as well as loving letters (in the beginning), from everywhere: Marseille to London. Often she included the number of the page she was on in *The Two Faces of Janus,* her new book, or how many pages she'd written of *Janus* that day. Gradually, there was questioning: Was I okay? Why didn't I write? Then there was cynicism: Was I already in love with someone new? Had I gone back to Kit? One letter was signed *Baffled. Love, Pat.*

I did not answer.

I still remember the way she opened her book *The Tremor of Forgery* (1969), with a New York writer in Tunisia unable to understand why his lover did not write him. He sent her a cable begging to know why she hasn't gotten in touch, and he signed it *Baffled. Love, Howard.*

Pat was gone almost three months when she sent a card inside a package.

On the front was a photograph of Salzburg with a greeting in German. *Frohe Weinacht und alles Gute im Neuen Jahr. With Love, Pat.*

On the back this message:

Dear MJ—
Another package that will come from Marseille is for you.
A package from Salzburg is for me—please hold.
Evidently, you're very busy, or my letters put you into a coma, probably the latter.
I hope you have a pleasant Christmas—with pleasant people, wherever you are. P.

There was a green Tyrolean jacket for me, too small, but cherished by the obsessed and guilty recipient.

At last I broke down and wrote her.

I believed that even Pat, with her very secretive side, would not mail a package to herself, in my care, if she was truly with someone else. Tom was also telling me I was letting someone slip away I'd regret losing.

"Make up your mind," I answered him. "You told me not to go to Europe with her."

"She'll come back," he said. "I saw how she was with you. You're both in too deep to cut away."

I wrote her as though nothing had happened, a loving letter, which she of course answered by asking what had taken me so long to get in touch.

Then the two packages arrived, in time for the holidays. The one for me, from Marseille, was a waiter's jacket, the kind she'd worn to Pete's when we had lunch with José Garcia Villa and his boyfriend.

I telephoned her. I knew she was spending Christmas in London.

I had not even sent her a Christmas present.

I lied and said I was saving it for when she returned. It was unpleasant to have an overseas conversation in those days. The wires crackled and you shouted just because it didn't seem likely you could talk from New York to London without shouting.

"Where have you been?" she persisted.

I said the truth. "I'd gone crazy imagining that you were with someone."

"I was with a lot of people."

"You know what I mean."

"And I thought Kit had moved back in with you. I was afraid to call."

"I was sure Mary was with you at some point."

"You were crazy. Are you over it now?"

"I think I am!"

"Get over it! I love you!"

"I love you, too. I'll write."

"You owe me a lot of letters."

"You'll get them," I promised.

Now speaking German very badly, I smoked Gauloises, and I worked half-heartedly on the hangover book with Polly. Ignoring all television and still slipping in an occasional call to hear Mary's voice, and to be sure she was not "over there" with Pat, I sent Pat notes across paper napkins from Peter's Backyard, the Jumbo Shop, Pete's, and the Algonquin Bar, a favorite haunt of Gold Medal editors and writers.

I had become as well as I could the person I had wished I could be those many years ago when we played Truth, and I said "Highsmith." The real truth was that I had become a fool, the worst kind of unselfconscious fool who had no clue she was one.

Tom complained that I sounded like Martha Wolfenstein when I talked, but I behaved like Pat.

A few weeks before Pat came back for her birthday on January 19th, I had dinner at Martha's. Nathan had sent from Paris an interview with Pat that had appeared in a French newspaper.

Martha translated for me, looking up in the middle of the interview to exclaim, "So she's a fan of Jouhandeau's? Nathan is, too."

I couldn't bring myself to tell Martha that very likely Pat had not read anything he'd written. She would have mentioned it to me. She was probably just trying to impress the French reporter.

Then Martha went back to the interview, only to exclaim again. "Robert Musil! Another of Nathan's favorites! I wonder if he read this, or just passed it along for you."

The idea of Pat's attempting to impress whoever wrote the piece endeared her to me somehow. It was something one of her fictional characters would do; it was something one of Vin Packer's characters would do, too. Even as I told myself never, never to use it against her in an argument, I knew that day would come.

Once Pat was home, I felt more anchored. She brought more presents and reassured me in every way she could that she loved me. I never told her that I'd tried to learn German, because I never wanted her to know how bad my foreign language disability was. I thought of old cartoon ads for learning to play the piano, popular when I was a kid. The heading was *They laughed when I sat down*, and then you would see this man playing, musical notes in balloons over the keys, astonished looks of surprise from onlookers. Is that what I'd thought, that I could learn to converse a little now and then with Pat, in German? The teacher would wince when I said even a word.

I explained away the fact I'd taken to smoking Gauloises by saying it would make life easier for us if we used the same brand.

"Except I'm smoking German cigarettes now," said Pat. "Did you *really* think of me when I was gone? I was sure I was just a passing fancy."

In February I took her to Nicholson's for a belated birthday dinner, and gave her a gold ring with *er* engraved inside it (to complete the *rememb* inside my ring), "MM/PH" underneath with "1/19/60."

She said she'd been reading the New York newspapers to bring herself back in touch. I complimented her on her review in the *Sunday New York Herald Tribune*, where columnist James Sandoe wrote: *I think the world of Miss Highsmith because while she has me in her firm grasp she is quite simply the world. Any questions?*

"Yes, but did you see what Boucher wrote? He even admitted he was burnt out."

The reviews we were talking about were of *This Sweet Sickness*.

Anthony Boucher, Sandoe's counterpart in the *New York Times*, had written …*probably only a professional reviewer in a heavy season would protest that she might have got the same result in something under 100,000 words.*

"I wasn't reading the papers for my reviews," said Pat. "I was trying to catch up with the news here. What's going on with the nigras?"

"You mean the Negroes?"

"You're not doing them any favor pronouncing it *Negro*. They call themselves niggers. I've heard them."

"Well, if you have it's different. We can call ourselves queers but when someone else does it, it's derogatory."

"I don't know anyone who calls herself queer," Pat said. "And there are plenty of restaurants that don't want us. We don't stage a sit-in. We just find someplace else to eat."

"Okay," I gave up. I didn't want to spoil the evening.

"You don't know the South," Pat said.

"I went to boarding school with all Southern girls."

"Virginians aren't really Southern."

"Are Texans?"

"Where the colored are concerned, we are."

I'd done a Gold Medal book about the Emmet Till wolf whistle case in Mississippi. A young Negro boy had allegedly whistled at a white woman and gotten himself lynched because of it. I'd called my book *Dark Don't Catch Me*. When Pat and I first met, I'd explained that the title came from a saying Negroes had: "Dark, don't catch me in this town!" It meant whites didn't like them in town after dark, and, in some small Southern towns, didn't even like them wearing neckties, dressing like whites, putting on airs.

I remembered Pat had nodded and said that she'd grown up with them in Fort Worth, and they had their own parts of town to be in. As for wearing neckties, none of them wanted to. Why would they want to?

So at Nicholson's I let her remarks pass. I knew Pat was always more in touch with the prejudice against black people in South Africa than against Negroes in America. You could never find any chauvinism in Pat, just the opposite.

Pat said she'd seen Janet Flanner in Paris. She said Janet and Natalia had a perfect arrangement: They let each other have a life apart, but they would spend their old age together. Janet, she said, had this beautiful French woman when she was in France.

"And you?"

She reached her hand toward mine, fingertips over fingertips, all we were courageous enough to manage in a place like Nicholson's. We were the only same-sex couple there, and I knew even that gesture made me blush. "I was afraid I'd lost you," Pat said. "I didn't think about anyone else."

I never quite believed Pat, ever since I'd come to learn of her love affair with Mary through Mia Fabrizzio. I'd realized then how capable she was of duplicity, like the characters in her books, and in mine.

She was amazed to hear that Polly and I had worked on a book together, that Dell Publishing was actually going to do it in oversized, paperback form: *A Guide to the Hangover,* by M. J. Meaker, illustrated by Polly Cameron. (Pg. 1: *If you are an average hangover victim, you will most likely find the hangover in your bed.... Pg. 2: If you are above average you will find it in a strange bed...* etcetera.)

"But how did you meet Polly?" Pat asked.

"She called me to see if I'd like to work with her on it." A lie. But Polly had agreed to say *she* looked *me* up, not the other way around. Polly knew what a desperate wretch I'd become because of Pat.

"And it's really going to be published?"

I was as surprised as Pat was. Polly, too. Dell Publishers were planning to hold it for a year and launch it in 1961 on New Year's Day, possibly on Dave Garroway's morning show.

Carol, in a Thousand Cities was due out in the summer.

"You've been busy," Pat said. "I'm almost through with *Janus.* It's a variation on the folie à deux thing."

The sharing of delusional ideas was a theme Pat and I had in common. In our version, usually two men became involved in a crime. Pat had done *Strangers on a Train,* in 1951, where two men swap murders. In 1954, as Vin Packer, I'd published a paperback fictional version of the infamous Fredan-Wepman case, in which a young man talks a friend into helping him kill his mother. To my horror, Gold Medal Books retitled it *Whisper His Sin*. My title had been *The Cyanide Cocktail Murder*.

It was a theme Pat and I would both return to again and again in our careers. Anthony Boucher, reviewer of crime novels for the *New York Times*, inspired by *Whisper His Sin*, called my attention to the Parker-Hulme case in New Zealand. Two girls committing parricide. Right before I met Pat, Gold Medal published this Packer as *The Evil Friendship*. In his review of the book (1958) Boucher called it "a Lesbian Loeb-Leopold," pronouncing Packer "as relentlessly tough-minded as any of the best 'hard-boiled' writers."

To my amazement decades later, the clever, imaginative one of the homicidal duo, Pauline Parker, grown up and rehabilitated, would turn out to be the famous mystery writer Anne Perry.

Thirteen

At the University of Missouri, I'd had a creative writing teacher named William Peden. He came to New York one weekend in March, and asked me if I'd like to go to a party at Whit and Hallie Burnetts'. The founders of *Story Magazine,* the discoverers of William Saroyan, they were known to me, of course. In the early '50s I'd submitted short stories to *Story.*

I asked Bill if I could bring a friend, and I told him about Pat.

He was delighted to escort us to 135 Central Park West, where the party was in progress at eight o'clock.

Pat had had a few cocktails before we taxied over to get her, and then many more shots of straight gin once we were there. But Pat always drank a lot. That was her way. And she'd always held it well.

She'd worn a black wool suit with a black sweater and heels—she looked chic and sure of herself. I always liked her looks in women's clothes, even though she claimed she hated wearing skirts. She was thin, tall, with that thick black hair, and she had good bones. Since she had returned from Europe she'd been smoking Roth-Haendle cigarettes, the German equivalent of Gauloises.

I was in a suit myself, with high heels, watching her across the room, thinking about being the one to go to bed with her at the end of the evening. Both the Burnetts were hovering near her.

It was a very "in group" gathering; everyone seemed to know everyone else.

People said hello to Bill, but he didn't leave me and join others. I was grateful for that. He was always very much the gentlemanly Virginian, soft-spoken, a biographer of Thomas Jefferson, an English professor interested in young writers. We talked about old days at Missouri, and he congratulated me on the fact I was earning my living solely as a writer.

"Look how far you've come in such a short time," he said. "You have that nice big apartment in the Village. You're a success in your field and you'll probably go on to publish in hardcover."

"That's what I want to do," I said. More than ever I wanted to, because of Pat. I felt that she thought I could do better than be a paperback writer. She would sometimes mention that she had begun writing comic book scenarios for *Superman* and *Batman* before she'd moved on to "serious things." I knew she didn't think paperbacks were serious. I did. To me the only difference was the form, and the fact I got twice what Pat did for one book. I was free to write on any subject I wanted, and when I did mystery/suspense, I was reviewed in the same *Sunday New York Times* column Pat was.

I wanted to figure out how to live on what hardcover paid, and estimate my chances of selling to hardcover. I wasn't Pat when it came to keeping my living expenses down. I had large apartments and summer cottages I could afford thanks to my sales, but I wondered if I'd have as large an audience when my books cost four and five dollars instead of twenty-five cents. Since I met Pat, I thought about that more and more.

Bill and I found a sofa in a corner. Friends of the Burnetts who knew Bill came by to talk for a bit. When we were alone, he told me he'd had a rather sad marriage in the past years, that his wife was an invalid, that there was very little social life for him. He said that was why he loved coming to New York, renewing friendships, talking with writers and publishers. He was staying a week. "Maybe we'll make a date for dinner," he said, "just the two of us." I told him I'd like that.

Suddenly in the middle of the party, I heard him say, "Whit's heard Highsmith is of the Sapphic persuasion. Did you know that?"

"Oh, who told him that?" I said, as though that was preposterous. I wondered if my face looked red. It felt hot. I was always uncomfortable with anyone from the past suspecting *I* might be gay.

"Whit says she is. He met her at this cultural *Time/Life* editor's, and she's also a lesbian."

I knew that Bill was talking about Rosalind Constable.

"Shall I go over and ask her?" I said.

Bill shrugged and smiled. "I told Whit *you* weren't. I told him you were gaga over this Hungarian Communist when you were at Missouri. Whatever happened to that fellow?"

That fellow was George Gaspar, the only man I'd ever loved, a more cerebral entanglement than a physical one.

"George escaped from Hungary, with his wife and kids, in 1953. I got a letter from him my mother forwarded. He was in Vienna, in a refugee home maintained by American Mennonites."

"You see how lucky you are that you never went to Budapest with him?"

"He never asked me," I said.

"You were lucky," Bill repeated. And then I saw Pat walking toward us, swaying just a little bit more than she ever did when she drank. Or maybe it's the heels, I thought. But no, she had that dizzy smile that sometimes appeared when she was really tight, and this loose, slaphappy body language. I'd seen it before: at Martha and Nathan's; at a Harper Brothers party for Joan Kahn, her editor; and at a party given by one of the psychiatrists who was Tom Baird's old friend.

Pat walked up to where Bill and I were sitting, not looking at Bill, leaning down to say, "You want to go home? I want to. I hope you want to."

She had a glass of gin in one hand that looked dangerously close to being spilled on me. I stood up, and Bill did, too.

I put my own drink down and said to Bill, "I think I'd better get her home," as though she was going somewhere I wasn't going. I took the glass from her hand and put it on the table. Then she took my hand.

"You could put her in a taxi," Bill said softly to me. "Do you want me to help? We can call down to the doorman."

Pat overheard and said, "She wouldn't do that to me." She looked down at me, pushing her hair back with her hand. Her eyes were watery and her voice was thick with affection. "You *wouldn't,* would you?"

I thought, Oh, the hell with it and said, "Not on your life."

"Oh, ho!" I heard Bill cry out, but I couldn't look back to see the expression on his face. I knew my cheeks were crimson. I knew some of the guests were staring at us. My paranoid mind informed me that Whit had told all of them

Pat was a lesbian, so that made me one, too. I was never tough enough to shrug it off.

The next day I told Pat about it. She didn't remember anything.

"I'm really sorry," she said. "I liked your friend, too. Do you think it will matter?"

"It'll be hard for him to call me, I think. Not because we're queers, but because he had no idea when he told me about you, that I was your lover."

"Call him," Pat said.

But I didn't. I didn't want to have to explain myself to Dr. Peden. I never saw him again.

Much later Pat would use Dr. Peden's remark as ammunition in an argument for living abroad. "Do you think anyone at a cocktail party in Paris or Rome would even mention something like that? How vulgar!"

"The problem is I'm embarrassed to be this queer lady," I said to Martha Wolfenstein one night while we were having dinner. We liked to eat at Maria, this unpretentious, quiet little bistro on East 52nd Street. It was possible to have good food there, with tables far enough apart to have privacy.

"Why are you whispering?" Martha asked.

"I just told you why." But no one could hear us. My voice often lowered automatically when I was on the subject in public.

"But it seems to me Pat puts you in embarrassing situations," said Martha. "Why does she want to do that?"

"She doesn't *want* to do it. She drinks too much when we go certain places."

"What kind of places?"

"Like your house. Like Whit Burnett's party. She's not easy around people she doesn't know, and you know how New York is: There's always a party, a dinner at someone's, cocktails. She's not a good drinker when it comes to things like that."

"You've said that before. You said it last summer and you've mentioned it a few times since she's been back."

"I think she panics at social situations, unless we're with people we know."

"Your own kind."

"Or people we know who don't give a damn what we are."

"Well, no one can blame her for that."

"But she claims she's not concerned whether people think she's gay or not."

Martha said, "Nathan and I have a colleague who's brilliant: a doctor, a psychiatrist. He can't belong to the New York Psychoanalytic Society, because he's a homosexual. At our parties he's very ill at ease. I've seen his hand shake holding a drink. All of his colleagues there belong to the N.Y.P.S., and they *know* why he's not a member, because why else wouldn't he be? It's the most prestigious organization in New York for analysts."

"How does this Society *know* he's gay?"

"Your own analyst has to swear you never had that problem or you can't get in. I doubt that Kurt's ever tried to belong; he knows what he's up against.... Anyway, he's usually so confident and autonomous. It always amazes us to see the effect that rejection has on him."

"Why does he go to your parties?"

"Maybe he doesn't realize how changed he is at them,

or maybe he's always trying to get past it, and make a better impression at the next party."

"So you think Pat's homosexuality really bothers her?"

"I think the way people view you bothers most homosexuals. How could it not?"

"Maybe Pat's right. It's easier in Europe. Maybe we should move there."

"First find out if you get along," said Martha. "For you, living in Europe is a big step."

When I got back to 13th Street, Pat was in the living room reading the newspapers. She'd been to dinner with José Garcia Villa. She was sober and glad to see me.

I was high. After Martha and I had killed a bottle of white wine with our chicken parmigiana, we'd had some Rémy Martin.

"I think we ought to leave New York," I said, "and I don't mean go to Europe."

"What *do* you mean?" She put down the *Times* and I sat beside her on the couch, taking her hand.

"Palisades?" I said. "Sneden's Landing?"

"Are you serious?" Her face beamed. "I'd love to get out of here! I can't work here!"

I sat there while she leaned over to kiss me, smiling, making plans to call Polly, to call someone she knew in real estate in Rockland County, her mind running with it: She'd have to find a way to break her lease on Irving Place.

"*You* won't have any problem," she said. "Landlords love to free up a rent-controlled apartment like this one.... Our cats will love living in the country! I'll love it! *We'll* love it!" She was on her feet. "Let's have a nightcap and celebrate! How about a splash of Lillet with some soda? I put a bottle on ice."

But I felt suddenly sick, sorry I'd mentioned it, and not sure I could do it. Leave New York? Most of my young life I'd imagined myself living in New York City.

I would never forget a 1956 coffee house reading of Walt Whitman, not a particular favorite until one night a young poet quoted his "Manhattan" in *Leaves of Grass: ...The beautiful city, the city of hurried and sparkling waters! the city of spires and masts! The city nested in bays! my city! The city of such women, I am mad to be with them! I will return after death to be with them!* I had just found my own gay crowd. I had just met Kit. I called up Tom and asked him if he had that poem by Whitman in his library, and he laughed and recited: *The city of such young men, I swear I cannot live happy, without I often go talk, walk, eat, drink, sleep, with them!*

What made me think I could live anywhere but New York City—never mind who I would be doing it for? What price glory?

Fourteen

The first week in July Pat and I went to Bucks County, Pennsylvania, in search of a house near New Hope. We were helped by Al and Betty Ferres, who went weekends to a small house in Point Pleasant. They were old friends of Pat, former neighbors from an apartment house she'd lived in when she first came to New York.

We stayed the night in the Black Bass Inn on the Delaware Canal. It was a charming old place run by a young gay man, who kept a candle burning on the mantle in the reception room, in memory of his partner, who'd been killed in a Christmas automobile accident.

The Inn was right for Pat: no television, but room service from the bar, and a lovely look from a balcony at old barges drifting down the water. Pat was having her "before dinner drink," busy sketching the landscape, while the owner of a house down the road came to interview us, as possible tenants. She was moving into the village of New Hope. The house was too big for her: four bedrooms, four rooms downstairs, ten acres mostly leased to neighboring farmers, but there were two acres free with a barn on it and pear and apple trees.

By noon we had signed a two-year lease, beginning September 1960. We were renting unfurnished, with the understanding we would also maintain the two acres, the house, barn, and fruit trees. It was understood, too, that all of it was listed for sale, and if a buyer came along we would show the house.

We would take possession on Monday, the 29th of August.

The names of the popular songs of that summer seemed prophetic to me: Ike and Tina Turner's "A Fool in Love," and Elvis Presley's "It's Now or Never."

It was a high/low summer in which I was high a lot and down a lot. Nathan was in Paris, so we visited Martha at Fair Harbor on Fire Island. While Pat spent hours sketching the ocean and the gulls, I walked the beach with Martha, determined not to tell her how ambivalent I felt about the move.

After dinner, late at night, I often stayed up drinking brandy with Martha while Pat went to bed.

"What do you two talk about?" Pat would ask me.

I never had an answer. We talked about everything. From the beginning of our friendship we had always been as comfortable with each other as old friends. We didn't *have* to talk; there were moments when we didn't, but mostly we talked together about books, things in the newspapers, and our lives. Sometimes she would talk to me about her patients, without identifying them. Most of them were children of psychoanalysts. The one I remembered the best was "the snake boy" whose psychiatrist father thought he had sadistic tendencies, because he fed his pets live mice and watched them eat.... I always asked Martha how he was doing, and ultimately I wrote a hardcover book called *Shockproof Sydney Skate* starring a teenager who wanted to be a herpetologist, and was competing with his lesbian mother for a Bryn Mawr girl.

Some thirty years later at Martha's memorial service, Margaret Mead whispered to me, "That's the snake boy," when a young man passed us. "He's a weatherman now," she said. "He tracks storms."

I knew that I didn't have to tell Martha how nervous I was about the move to Pennsylvania. She sensed it. She would remind me that it was an easy commute from Trenton, New Jersey, into Manhattan, Trenton being the nearest railroad station to New Hope. She would talk about the symbolic name: New Hope. She would sound enthusiastic about getting away from the city for an occasional visit in the country on weekends. But she also said it was going to be lonely for her without me. Most of her friends were coupled.

Except for Peggy Lewis, an acquaintance of Pat's right in the village of New Hope, Pat knew no one in the vicinity besides Al and Betty. They went to Bucks County to escape people and have some quiet time, so we would not meet anyone through them. We wouldn't see that much of them, either, for the same reason.

I knew no one there.

We were not located in the village of New Hope. We were seven miles away, the nearest hamlet being Point Pleasant, which had a big used furniture barn and a gas pump. Doylestown, Pennsylvania, was about fifteen miles away.

I believed the lack of nearby friends and the isolation would be good for us. Pat was sure of it. Somehow when we spoke of beginning our life together in New Hope, Pat had managed to exact a promise from me: If we didn't like where we were at the end of our lease, we'd give Europe a try. If we did like Bucks County, then we'd renew the lease and take a few months off to travel in Europe.

Another reason I felt good about the move was that I had read *This Sweet Sickness* shortly after Pat left for Europe. Her hero, David Kelsey, also went by the name William Neumeister. Pat chose her names for characters very carefully, and it was no accident that Kelsey's other persona meant "new master" in German.

Kelsey was one of her craziest creations: a man so in love with a woman that he bought a house and furnished it for her, while she was married to someone he would eventually have to murder. My favorite scene came near the end, when he imagined that he took his beloved Annabelle to dinner at Romeo Salta on West 56th Street. He ordered dinner for them: but first a daiquiri for her phantom presence, and a martini for himself. The waiter did as he was told: put the daiquiri on the plate next to him. Then after David enjoyed another, talking aloud to Annabelle as he envisioned her having her second cocktail (which of course he drank), he ordered dinner for them. Clams, veal piccata, a mixed salad, and a bottle of Valpolicella.

All the while he talked to Annabelle he heard the sound of laughter in the restaurant, and saw people smiling at him. When the check was presented he had only eight dollars and he owed $16.37. After he wrote a check he realized the waiter recognized his name. David Kelsey was a wanted man, and now he must run…and so he did, ultimately losing track of Annabelle, and finding himself on the ledge of an apartment building, wanting to jump. He imagined that Annabelle was down in the crowd, wearing a white coat, hard to see through the darkness. Then he stepped off "into that cool space, that fast descent to her, with nothing in his mind but a memory of a curve of her shoulder, naked, as he had never seen it."

I loved the book, at the same time realized the pull of Mary Ronin, who had inspired it. I envied Pat's passionate and romantic heroes. They were always male, and always the answer to Auden's plaintive request that if equal loving could not be, let the more loving one be he. I wanted to be loved that way as well as to write about loving that way. But first I wanted to be with Pat away from New York, away from Mary Ronin, and away from all temptation.

By August, Pat still had not found a way to break her lease on Irving Place. Tom was coming up from Washington and the three of us were going to spend a weekend at Fair Harbor, since Martha was attending a conference.

Pat said I should go ahead, that José Garcia Villa had a friend who could help her get rid of her Irving Place apartment.

"Will he sublet?"

"I don't want that," said Pat. "I want to break the lease."

"How?"

"He'll say he's going to sublet," Pat said. "They'll break the lease then and there."

"Why would they?"

"Because he's a Nee-gro." She always exaggerated the pronunciation since I'd corrected her.

"Doesn't that humiliate him?"

"He makes money that way," Pat said. Then she sighed, always ready to be blamed for some wrongdoing. That seemed to be a part of Pat's personality when she was with a woman. She said, "I suppose you don't approve."

"I don't care, if it'll get us to New Hope."

The day Tom and I went to the island, Martin Luther King, Jr., was leading protests against Georgia law that allowed department stores to continue to segregate their lunch counters and restrooms. Pat had been grumbling about Northerners not understanding "the colored."

On the ferry from Bay Shore I complained that Pat was too southern in ways she thought about Negroes.

We were bumping through the waves when Tom said, "Stop trying to reform everybody. I remember how mad I'd get when you wouldn't laugh at some of my jokes, just because they were about Sammy and Isidore."

"It was never Isidore," I said. "It was always Izzy. Sammy and Izzy."

"Christ, I bet you don't even know the difference between a motet and a madrigal. Do I complain that you're vastly ignorant about music?"

"I know a madrigal is a song just for voices, no instruments," I replied.

"A motet is similar but its subject matter is religious," said Tom. "Pat's from Texas. She's trying to overcome it but you're no help. You won't even travel anywhere with her."

"I am leaving New York because of her," I reminded him.

"And she'll never hear the end of it."

"I'm going to try hard to change when we get to New Hope," I said. "I don't want to be a henpecker."

"I'll keep my eye on you," he said.

He waited until dinner to tell me. He'd bought an expensive burgundy and wanted us both to have wine glasses in our hands so that we could lean across the table, clink them, and wish ourselves luck.

I was starting a life with Pat.

Tom was leaving the National Gallery to write, not the long-awaited Ph.D. thesis, but a novel. A friend had found him a house in Princeton, New Jersey.

"I'll be your neighbor again," said Tom.

Fifteen

Why are you putting yourself out of the running? my father wrote about my move with Pat. *You won't meet any men in rural Pennsylvania.*

Unlike my father (who refused to believe my mother's "gossip" about me), my mother never spent a moment in denial when it came to accepting anything she discovered was wrong with me.

> *Of course you will not see me again unless you come home ALONE, for I will never come to one you share with a woman that way. You are probably wise to move as far away from normal people as possible, since now you are all but wearing a sign around your neck saying what you have become!*

A Greenwich Village moving company called The Mothertruckers took the furniture from both apartments.

We filled my small British Ford convertible with my five cat cases containing Mousey, Mr. Schwartz, Kelly, Peter Lewis, and Lovelove, as well as Pat's canvas bag bearing Spider.

Pat had brought some small pots of African violets to my apartment, too, but we could not fit them into the car. Nor could we fit in a hanging fern. There was not room left for anything.

Pat was weeping for her houseplants as she got behind the wheel.

"I've had them for years. Even when I was away on long trips I always saw that they were cared for."

Pat had already sent two boxes of plants with The Mothertruckers.

Our new life began with Pat's tears; feline hissing, spitting, and moaning from the back seat of the car; and on one of the hottest days of the year (no air conditioning in the car, of course) an hour and a half delay in the Holland Tunnel.

Back on the road, Pat smoked and frowned and wished we could at least stop for lunch and a glass of wine. I insisted we continue: it was too hot for the cats...and we drove on, arriving at our empty house with the movers still not there. Of course, *they* probably did stop for lunch and drinks.

We let the cats loose in the big upstairs of the house, putting out litter for them, food, and water. Pat went in to New Hope and fetched a loaf of bread, hard salami, cheese, mustard, and a bottle of cold Soave she'd bought and had opened at a liquor store. She'd picked up paper plates, cups, and napkins. She always carried a switchblade, so we had our knife. We sat on the front porch looking over a field of lush, green, uncut grass, relaxing at last, listening to a portable radio I'd put in the Ford's trunk. There was a memorial in progress for Oscar Hammerstein II, who'd just died. They were playing songs from some of his Broadway hits he'd written with Richard Rodgers. Pat was grinning at me as we listened to "Some Enchanted Evening."

"Once you have found her," she sang to me, "never let her go."

The sky was becoming an early evening deep blue, with streaks of red. Way, way down the road, a light went on in the small one-floor farmhouse where an old couple lived named the Knappenburgers. They were our only neighbors on Old Ferry Road, RFD New Hope. They were Pennsylvania Dutch, our landlady had told us, their children grown and gone.

I was watching Pat light one Roth-Haendle from another, look out across the fields, touching my arm now and then with her long fingers, listening with me to the music from the radio.

I was thinking that one of the things I loved about her was that she took things in stride. Okay, so The Mothertruckers were long overdue, and it would be dark before long. She didn't exclaim or complain. Through it all she was affectionate.

"You know what I think?" she said while I was thinking that. "I think you're the calmest woman I've ever known."

"Right now I'm the happiest, too."

"I'm happier," she chuckled. Sometimes when I'd tell her that I loved her, she'd say, "I love you more."

I decided I'd always remember how our life together began, the two of us sitting on the porch, that blue/red sky, and a warm summer wind just beginning.

Then we heard the rumbling of a truck and Pat said, "I bet that's them."

From the upstairs, one of the cats began to try to intimidate another with a piercing yowl punctuated by the sound of a roll-over scuffle, several cat voices raised in a menacing chorus.

I ran to separate them.

The Mothertruckers turned down our drive, honking the horn, the sides of their rickety van bulging with our belongings.

Sixteen

Pat was the first person I'd ever lived with who was there all the time. I learned on our first real night together that she understood the rhythm of a relationship far better than I did. After we'd spent a day arranging our furniture (our work spaces and our bedroom took priority), she'd made a stew that was cooking on the stove. She called up to me that she was making martinis for the cocktail hour. Unlike Pat, I'd come downstairs without changing from old jeans and a sweater. She had bathed, put on her gray flannel pants and a white shirt with dark ascot, and shined her loafers.

I imagined that we would finally have a chance to sit down, admire our new living room, and make small talk: our first quiet time together since the night before when The Mothertruckers had left us with our belongings stuffed into three rooms downstairs.

I felt bad that I hadn't showered myself and put on clean clothes.

At first I thought Pat had taken note of my dishabille and taken umbrage as well.

She handed me my drink, then, saying she'd see me at dinner, walked into her study and shut the door.

I soon learned that this was her time to read the dictionary, which she did every night before dinner, enjoying her second martini. The first she had sipped while she made dinner.

The time we spent at dinner was to be the fixed time we spent together every day. Other times would be unplanned, accidental, unpatterned. Sometimes in the early evening she'd say, "Let's make walking drinks and admire the property."

Sometimes on our walks the corn on the leased acres adjoining ours was so high we could only see the sky. Both of us were sorry we didn't know the names of many of the trees and flowers and wildlife. In school I'd learned the great rivers of India were the Indus, the Ganges, the Mahanadi, and the Kistna. I'd learned that most of the sugar we use comes from sugar cane and is known as sucrose. But I never knew what to call the common birds in our backyard or the huge trees in the woods at the end of the street. My parents had no curiosity about nature. And Pat, who grew up mostly in New York City, felt as ignorant as I was about the same things. She asked me to bring her some books on birds and trees and flowers when I went to the library. Soon, as we took our "walking drinks" and looked around, Pat would point out seckel pears and smokehouse apples, zinnia and marigolds, and goldfinches feasting on the seeds in sunflowers. She'd point out milkweed pods that were about to burst and send little parachutes up. Both of us loved learning those things, but Pat was the more diligent researcher. I liked that she made more of our lives, not just with the occasional walks, but in other, thoughtful ways: the fresh orange juice by my plate in the morning, the time she took to brush my cats, the surprises she'd leave at my typewriter—a Hershey kiss, a book of Renée Vivien's poetry, with a red autumn leaf marking the page where a poem began *You will come, your eyes full of night and of yesterday....*

At dinner we always killed a bottle of wine, so I was slightly smashed each evening, until I learned not to have a cocktail hour. The wine with our meal was enough for me. Pat was much better at handling gin and wine, and sometimes also a brandy after dinner while she reread the pages she'd written that day. Unlike Pat, once I did my work, I put it away until the following day.

Pat was worried about *The Two Faces of Janus*. She was just putting finishing touches on it. I remember our dinner conversations those early days together, because our discussions of "themes" proved to be an epiphany for me. She was worried that the two male characters in *Janus* somehow didn't work, that there was not enough reason for their bonding.

"It's that theme," I said. "It's that two-man relationship again. I'm having trouble myself, because I'm repeating that theme."

I was working on a suspense story called *Something in the Shadows*, setting it where we lived in Pennsylvania. On a whim, I was using my own surname for my main character. The story concerned Joseph Meaker and a man named Hart, who ran over Meaker's beloved cat in his Mercedes. Hart did it deliberately, Meaker believed, and he befriended Hart to find out what Hart prized, bent on destroying it for revenge.

"Don't tell me the plot," Pat said, "just tell me why it bothers you that you're repeating the theme."

"Why am I always gnawing on the same old bone?"

"Because that's your bone. Use it. You never really repeat as much as you do fine-tune something that's innate."

Our talking about it made me able to dive back into the book enthusiastically, instead of worrying every other day if I was Johnny-one-note. I would go on eventually to develop other themes, but I no longer became self-conscious when that one returned, as it would in whatever disguise I chose, whether suspense, fantasy, or young adult writing.

That, and other things about our beginning days, made me believe I had found the right person, and the right place…that as wonderful as New York City was for a young person, now I was beginning my thirties, and I had found my lifetime partner. We didn't need the excitement and variety of New York. We didn't need its ubiquitous distractions either.

Pat, who had never watched television before, made a concession and watched a half hour of nightly news with me. There was trouble in the Belgian Congo, and stories of it featured President Joseph Kasavubu. This inspired Pat to name our house, and one afternoon as I returned from Doylestown where I did the grocery shopping, I saw the sign out front: CASAVUBU.

That was typical of Pat's humor. She loved plays on names, and collected wedding notices, when, for example, a Miss Driwell would marry Mr. Fountain, or Miss Master would marry Mr. Bateson. She had an almost British love of humor that had to do with bodily functions. Anything suggesting farting or peeing or defecating would crack her up.

Our landlady made Pat remove the handmade sign one afternoon when she came on a visit about another matter. After all, the house was on the market, and no one she knew thought it was funny, anyway, once it was explained.

The other matter was the disappearance of hunters' pheasants, left in a parked truck on Old Ferry Road. Had we seen anything? As a longtime former resident, and now landlady of one prominent house on the road, she had been asked by the police for any information about us, or anything we might have told her.

We invited her in for a cocktail, and lied easily, saying we had no idea what had happened to those hunters' pheasants. In fact we had filched all three and buried them inside our barn. Pat had even hesitated to sketch the beautifully colored feathers of one, before she dug its grave, wondering if making use of its death was not far from killing it for a meal.

We had come to hate the hunters, their raucous noise, their little-boy enthusiasm and special gear, as they marched off to put some gorgeous bird to death. We had watched them from our windows, chug-a-lugging from pints, rowdy, unshaven specimens of Neanderthal man.

They always went back into the woods, after leaving behind their first catch: rabbits, squirrels, more often pheasants. We knew they were going back for deer. We had seen the bloody animals hanging from their truck after a day with guns.

The hunters parked in the opposite direction of the Knappenburgers. No one could see us without intention and binoculars.

Pat suggested to our landlady that the hunters' pheasants might have been a drunken fantasy, since we smelled whiskey on their breaths when they'd knocked on our door asking if *we'd* seen anyone near their truck.

Our landlady said, "They wouldn't *both* think they'd caught pheasant even if they were drinking."

"It could be folie à deux," Pat said, and served a second strong martini to our guest while she explained the concept of simultaneous insanity.

I'm sure *that*, combined with Casavubu, was enough reason for our landlady to telephone henceforth, rather than drop by.

It suited us.

No one dropped by.

I missed the sight and sound of kids. My one regret about not being heterosexual was not being able to have children. An organization called Foster Parents was popular then, and Pat and I joined, letting the sex and nationality of "our child" be decided for us. For twenty-five dollars a month we supported Cha in a Korean orphanage—under Christian sponsorship, I suspected. Seven-year-old Cha's letters would arrive with the jubilant greeting "How in Christ are you?"

If yesterday had been at all like today, I suppose I'd have talked Pat into some Chinese babies. That would have made our life perfect…but we had to satisfy ourselves with saving critters who came through the animal door in a cat's mouth, writing our novels, cooking for each other, and swooning over the new landscape, the smell of the country, the rich sight of the sun rising or descending, and our love for each other.

Every day including weekends, I would sleep late, while Pat made herself breakfast. Then I'd drive to Doylestown to buy the *New York Times,* and to have something to eat at a luncheonette or a soda fountain, or in the front room of a small house on the road, where Mennonites served food and next door did laundry. I liked to stop there most of all, and except for Pat's white shirts, which she preferred to wash and iron herself, I took all of our clothes and linens there.

Our schedules meshed nicely. I was an afternoon worker, so just as I had in Manhattan, I ate lunch out. A morning worker, Pat was usually finished with her day's stint, and a lunch she'd made for herself, by the time I got home. She would be gardening or making furniture just as I was climbing the stairs to my study.

Occasionally, on weekends, when I passed the Knappenburgers' house, I saw their two grandchildren. They were ages nine and eleven, they had told me once when I stopped to buy lemonade from them. They would always wave wildly at my car. There wasn't any automobile like it in Bucks County. It was a lavender-colored British Ford, with a white cloth top that had three positions: closed, three-quarters closed, or all the way down. I liked to keep it three-quarters closed, the equivalent of today's sun roof.

Sometimes these little girls would set up a card table in the front yard and sell cider, toll house cookies, pies, and pussy willows. I'd stop and buy a drink and a sweet, and they'd tell me about their favorite subjects in school, a Friends school, since they were Quakers.

I liked talking to them, and taking the baked goods home for our dessert.

One warm autumn Sunday morning, the only day Pat and I didn't work, we were enjoying a late breakfast in our kitchen. Pat was wearing just her white pajama bottoms, and I, barefoot as she was, had on a knee-length silk nightshirt. We had stopped as we were cleaning up, to kiss and caress each other.

I heard the giggling first and, breaking away from Pat's arms, saw the older girl's glasses catch the sun, saw them turn their backs and run down our side steps, then watched as they ran their bikes down the long length of our drive-way, one falling, the other helping her up to a wobbling getaway: They flew from whence they came, all the way down Old Ferry Road.

On the porch, in front of the glass storm door that had been open, they had left a loaf of fresh baked banana bread, wrapped in a paper towel.

I called Mrs. Knappenburger to thank them for sending us a treat and she said, "You're welcome, I guess." She hung up as I started to ask her how she and Mr. Knappenburger were.

After that, I never saw much of the kids. They seemed to disband their roadside business. Since my car was easy to spot from a distance, if they were outside visiting on a weekend, they made a fast retreat into the house before I passed by.

Pat made many jokes about how our lewd behavior must have traumatized "the poor dears," and she made up a dirty limerick about the incident that began, "One sunny day on our bikes / we drove down the road to the dykes'...."

I laughed about their aborted visit, too, but I also felt both sadness and anger. I remembered Pat telling me of two lesbians who moved in together at Sneden's Landing, how they put a timer in one of the upstairs bedrooms, so that the neighbors would notice the lights on in both bed-rooms, and believe they had separate rooms. It was easier in a city for same-sex couples who could choose to ignore neighbors, but, in a small town, hard to keep your private life private.

I waited for the moment, sure to come, when Pat would tell me that small children in Paris or Rome would think nothing of seeing something like that.

Seventeen

I remember how I enjoyed writing *Something in the Shadows*. When I write suspense, I often have my hero interested in something I know little about, so I have engaging research. In one of my books a lead character carved the saints out of soap, and another was a handwriting analyst who also collected autographs. Therefore I learned about Saint Lucy, who was told so often by a nobleman her eyes were beautiful, that she finally tore them out in desperation, and ultimately became the patron saint of those afflicted in the eyes. I also learned to beware of feather-edged handwriting, and writing with letters broken at the base.

Because I had moved to Pennsylvania Dutch country, my hero, Joseph Meaker, became fascinated with hex signs and symbols like the star motif in Berks County, and the flower pattern favored by the farmers around Lehigh and Northampton. Meaker had received a grant from the Pennsylvania Society of Folk Mores. He and his wife had just moved to Old Ferry Road, outside New Hope.

Grief-stricken over the killing of his precious Siamese cat, Ishmael, he began to hate the jolly hunters who came on adjoining property to kill squirrels, rabbits, and deer. He even stole one of their pheasants and buried it.

When he was not investigating hexerei, or planning revenge on the man who ran over the Siamese, he was reliving a past love affair.

I used all my experience with the Communist Party, at the University of Missouri. I changed my Hungarian lover,

George, into a female named Varda, whom Meaker's wife liked to call "Varnish." Varda was the love of his life, and he relived the day, in 1948, when presidential candidate Henry Wallace came to the Missouri campus, how the Communists used him. They arranged to have a Negro teacher/speaker shouted down and pelted with garbage at a Wallace rally. The attackers were not students, but the newspapers believed they were, and the following day all the Missouri papers and even the *New York Times* wrote editorials decrying the incident. Great publicity for Wallace at the expense of the university. This was a true story, and I used George's background, and his letters, as I had Varda justify what had happened. Shades of "the end justifies the means."

I had never written anything about George in the thirteen books I'd published before I met Pat. I believed that I was beginning to review my past, the way someone might who had married and turned down a new road. I imagined that there was a new energy, and I gave all the credit for this to my sweet, peaceful life with Pat.

I didn't miss New York City. We had arrived just as the yellow goldenrod and the soft blue wild aster colored the untilled fields. The corn was high, the air was filled with the perfume of ripe grapes. Near our barn were apples and pears ready for the picking, and overhead we'd see great clouds of blackbirds gathering to head south. Everything about nature seemed sharper that autumn, probably because I had been city-pent so long.

We usually saw only one person a week, someone who came from New York—Rosalind Constable, Kit, or José Garcia Villa—or perhaps Tom driving over from Princeton.

Once a month we saw the Ferreses, who weekended in Bucks County. Martha Wolfenstein had Nathan with her from France, and he wanted to be in New York, so for a while she did not come.

I was also, in my spare time, making notes for the suicide book, and researching prospective subjects. I still remember our first snowstorm in early November, not caring that at dinner, by candlelight in our kitchen, my car outside was already covered. The forecast was grim. But Pat had made sauerbraten, which we drank with a bottle of Bordeaux, a fire going (it was a house of four chimneys), and on the table an exhibition catalogue from Kootz Gallery of Arshile Gorky. Nearby was the autobiography of Gorky I'd just finished, written by Ethel Schwabacher. Gorky's theme, according to Schwabacher, was *liebestod,* or love-death. A suicide in 1948, age forty-four, Gorky had hung nooses about his property in Connecticut, until the day he finally hanged himself.

Before dinner Pat and I had looked at some of his paintings in the catalogue, and during dinner talked about the three crucial defeats he'd suffered near the end of his life: his wife's plan to leave him, a fire destroying his work, and a broken neck.

"I could probably recover from the first and last," said Pat, "but not the second."

"I couldn't take any of it," I said.

We opened a second bottle of wine that night. Part of it was the storm and the idea we'd go nowhere for a few days, probably, and part of it was the relief that *Janus* had finally been sent off to Joan Kahn at Harper Brothers. Pat was both restless and relaxed, foregoing her solitary nightly reading of the dictionary. We'd recently traveled to Philadelphia to buy her a piano, which she played badly, although determined to practice and improve. Her grandmother had played, and Pat had learned when she was a child.

Finishing the book had also given her time to do some carpentry, which she dearly loved doing: making a three-legged stool, planning a table and a bookcase.

At dinner that night she said, "This is the first time I've ever finished a book without having a trip planned."

I held my breath waiting for a next sentence, for an accusation or a lament, or perhaps another paean to Paris and Rome, Marseille and Positano. Since both of us had been drinking a lot that night, I wouldn't have been surprised to hear her complain mournfully, and to hear me defend angrily.

But Pat's next sentence was about how satisfied she was with life, how strange it was that love solved so much, including wanderlust.

You remember so few moments in the best or worst of times; so few moments are recorded with the room you were in, the food you were eating, what you were talking about and feeling. That snowy night at the end of fall, 1960, was a time that stayed in my memory. I remember thinking that I had never come that close to having everything I wanted.

Two days later, we had to call someone to plow the long road from Old Ferry Road down to our house. We were told by the landlady to call Move Away in Point Pleasant. They had the equipment, and it was what they did in winter when few people planned moves.

We were sprung just in time to drive to Trenton and meet the train Mr. and Mrs. Shepard Rifkin would arrive on. Pat seemed not at all surprised that Ellen Hill had married, and that Rifkin was a writer.

As we drove along slippery roads to fetch them, Pat had a slanted grin, and she reminded me, "Ellen always said she wasn't homosexual, that she liked good food too much for that."

Rifkin was younger (my age, I guessed), with thick spectacles, more hair on his legs and arms than on his head, and a hearty friendliness. He was the type who never took off his baseball cap. Pat had made short ribs and boiled buttered potatoes with parsley for dinner, preceded by many martinis for them, and none for me. I barely sipped a glass of Bordeaux. I was determined to be at my best, since Ellen was so judgmental and haughty.

Pat had made funnel cakes for dessert, from an old Pennsylvania Dutch recipe she'd found. She served them drizzled with a mixture of rum and confectioner's sugar. We carried them into the living room to have with coffee.

Later, while I was cleaning up in the kitchen, Shep came in to keep me company. He said we should let them reminisce, and said it was a shame to waste the fire. He slipped another log on the embers and poured himself a brandy.

We talked for a long time about places we liked in Greenwich Village. When he said he liked a restaurant named Potpourri, I asked him if he knew Lorraine Hansberry, who'd written the successful play *A Raisin in the Sun.* She was the first female Negro playwright who'd made it to Broadway, and she was also a closeted lesbian.

"Sure, that's Bob's wife," said Shep. Robert Nemiroff's family owned Potpourri, and Lorraine had worked there waiting tables.

"How do you know Lorraine?" Shep asked.

I said something about meeting her at a party. I didn't tell him I'd never met her husband, or that I didn't know her in that context. I knew her lover, and her gay friends. In those days we didn't "out" one another. There were all sorts of ways we hid our connections to each other so that people who knew we were homosexuals wouldn't know others were. I can remember a night when David Susskind, a top TV producer, came into the Grand Tichino in Greenwich Village, his female assistant with him. We all knew Jackie. One of us at our table of five lesbians had had an affair with her, and I'd joined her table at gay bars many times. None of us looked their way. Mum was the word in a situation like that, always.

After I finished the dishes, I sat down beside Shep on the bench at the table in front of the fireplace. I was stone cold sober, so I poured myself a brandy, and another for him. We talked about agents. At that time I didn't have a literary agent. I did all the negotiating by myself, which belongs in the same category as a lawyer acting as his own lawyer, and having a fool representing him. Shep was thinking of going with Donald MacCampbell. Did I know anything about his agency?

"If you *do* know anything about it," coming from the doorway, from Ellen's angry mouth, "save it until tomorrow, if you would be so kind, Marijane!"

It was obvious she'd been standing just outside the door listening.

"What's the matter, honey?" Shep asked.

"What's the matter? I'm in bed by myself and my new husband is down here drinking with some woman who claims men don't interest her, so what is this little charade before the fire?"

"Honey," he was on his feet, crossing to her, "we're just writers talking about writing stuff."

"I'm just a woman shut off by myself in the freezing upstairs, and a lot you care!"

I closed up while Shep followed her upstairs with the posture of a child being tugged to bed by his ear, even though he towered over Ellen.

Pat was chuckling when I crawled in beside her.

"Why don't we make a lot of noise, like we're making love?" she said.

They were right down the hall in the Rose Room. Wallpaper splashed with roses covered not only the walls, but the ceiling as well, and there were a bedspread and lampshades in the same pattern. When we moved in we had teased that anyone who couldn't make up after a fight, and left the other to sleep on it, would be banished to the Rose Room.

I said, "Excuse me, but *how* did she land him? He's so gentle."

"That's me, as well," said Pat. "How did she land me?"

Eighteen

Sometimes a book will write itself. It seems to be on some tape in your head, and it comes forth unbidden, flows like a flood onto the page. That is one of the thrills of writing because, as any professional can tell you, it is the glorious exception.

I've found that such books happen when I'm writing about people and places either powerful in my memory, or new. In *Something in the Shadows*, both elements were at work. I think Meaker was truly Pat, brooding and melancholy, and that I was the brash advertising woman he'd married. Varda was George. It was all a wonderful hodgepodge of my new life and my old, and after a few months of research, it wrote itself in seven weeks.

By December, both Pat and I had books under consideration. We both felt good about them, too, but, being typical writers, we weren't without misgivings. Still, we were going through the same thing. That had never happened to me before. And misery *did* enjoy company.

We took advantage of our free time, driving to Doylestown to see movies, treating ourselves to dinner at the Black Bass, going to Princeton for dinner and overnight with Tom, and inviting friends out for whole weekends instead of merely one night.

The first weekend in December, Martha Wolfenstein came. Pat made a sumptuous turkey dinner, with mashed potatoes and gravy, cornbread stuffing, frozen peas, and cranberry sauce. She'd also baked a mince pie for dessert.

We drank and feasted and drank, and finally Pat said with a great yawn and stretch (it was about one A.M.) that she was going to bed.

Martha said nothing.

I felt obliged to sit with her and drink and talk, to more or less prove to her that my move away from New York had not affected our friendship. My love for Pat was not going to interfere. I knew this wouldn't go over well with Pat. She had always been jealous of Martha, and she had never understood what two people had to talk about for so long.

It was nearly two o'clock when Martha finally blurted out, "Nathan's leaving me!"

Then she told me in angry, crass, un-Martha-like language that a young French girl had seduced him, that he paid her to "suck his cock."

It was just at that point that Pat appeared on the staircase, *suck his cock* reverberating in the downstairs. Pat mumbled "Excuse me" over her shoulder, went into the kitchen, got ice in a glass, and flew back upstairs without another word.

Martha was too distraught to care about Pat.

"I found a telegram she sent him. Just three words. *Natan, Natan, Natan.*"

I kept saying how sorry I was.

"Couldn't you tell?" she said.

"Couldn't I tell what?"

"That something was wrong? Couldn't you tell when we talked on the phone, when I kept making excuses for not visiting, when you first saw me in the Trenton train station? Couldn't you tell something was horribly wrong?"

"I'm sorry that I couldn't."

"I must be a damn good actress! That little bitch has ruined my life!"

It was nearly three-thirty by the time I got to bed. I never believed that Pat was asleep, but she appeared to be. I'm sure she felt great disdain for this brilliant woman I admired who sat up with me discussing cocksucking until the early morning hours. Pat wouldn't want to make a scene, however. The opposite of me, she held things in.

I could hear Martha sobbing in the Rose Room. It was a very muffled sound, as though she was crying into her pillow. But Spider Highsmith heard it. His little black head came forth from the covers and he crept down to the end of the bed to listen. He sat on his haunches with his ear bent in that direction until I fell asleep.

The next day, almost afternoon, I managed to drag myself downstairs. As always, Pat had left a glass of fresh-squeezed orange juice for me.

Martha was sitting in the living room reading a book about A. E. Housman, a poet she was contemplating writing about.

Pat had served breakfast to her, then gone outside to chop wood.

When I went out to tell Pat I was taking Martha with me to shop and have lunch in Doylestown, she said, "Have fun. Although your friend isn't in a very fun mood."

"Pat, her husband left her."

"Is that what that was all about last night?"

"Nathan's left her and she feels horrible."

"Are turkey leftovers okay for dinner?"

I tried to give her a kiss, but she was peeved, not angry but miffed.

On the way to Doylestown, Martha said, "I don't think Pat takes to me."

"Well, there's where you're very wrong," I said with the hyperbolic tone that comes from bending over backward. And next from my mouth, "In fact, Pat just asked me if you'll have Christmas with us."

Nineteen

Sometimes you meet someone only three or four times, but that person will stay with you for years, and ultimately become a book.

Pat and I spent Christmas 1960 with just such a person.

Fearful that I had ruined the first Christmas we would spend together, I planned to call Martha after she got home and tell her the truth: that the invitation had been my idea alone, and that Pat had already accepted a Christmas invitation for us.

The latter was true. Without confirming it with me, Pat had told Al and Betty Ferres that we would go with them to the Porters, a couple I'd never met and Pat had only met once or twice. One of the ways Pat and I were alike was that it was hard for her to say no if she felt obligated. Pat thought that if it hadn't been for Al and Betty, we would never have found our place in Bucks County.

All of this came out as Pat and I had dinner together, after we put Martha on the train. We had planned to dine at the Black Bass Inn, on River Road, where we had stayed when we were looking for a house. We were refused entry to the dining room, since we were both in pants. Instead, we went into New Hope and ate at Chez Odette. Then it was the only glitzy bar/restaurant in the vicinity, sitting right on the Delaware.

I apologized for inviting Martha to Christmas and said I would get us out of it.

Pat apologized for accepting the dinner invitation at

the Porters', and said perhaps we could make it all work. She was sure Martha could be included, and so—one of her resigned shrugs—we would all be together.

"Martha probably won't even like the Porters," I said.

"No one likes Bud," Pat said. "But Hedda's tolerable.... Anyway, beggars can't be choosers."

"Martha didn't beg for an invitation. It was my idea."

"She made it impossible for you not to ask her," Pat said with her usual testiness when it came to Martha.

"I'm going to cancel Martha," I said.

"As you wish," Pat said, "but we still have to go to the Porters. I gave my promise to Al and Betty."

When we got home, our disgruntled mood changed abruptly as we discovered the case of wine waiting for us. The United Parcel delivery man knew we kept our side door unlocked for packages, since we had very ingenious raccoons on the property.

The wine had been sent to Pat by the Romeo Salta restaurant, with a note of thanks for being mentioned in *This Sweet Sickness*.

"It's a very fine Chianti," Pat said, "an expensive one."

"We'll probably have to try it out immediately," I said.

"I think you're right," said Pat.

While we enjoyed the bounty, with the six cats sitting in the living room with us, Pat told me about the Porters.

Pat's version of the Porter marriage was that Bud had married Hedda for her money. Bud, according to Pat, was a secret homosexual who taught at City College and entertained male students at his Greenwich Village apartment. Al Ferres had told Pat about it.

"Does Hedda know?"

"Hedda only cares for her dogs. I can't remember the breed now, it's rare and they cost a fortune. She spends all her time at shows and back in her kennel, where she even has a sitting room she reads in and hooks rugs in."

Pat took a swallow of wine, grinning evilly now, warming to the idea of a bizarre Christmas gathering. "Then there's Hedda's face. It's very red, like her hands when they're not bandaged. She's allergic to everything. One weekend years ago I stayed with Al and Betty. Bud was out in Arizona visiting his family. Betty invited Hedda over for dinner and she scratched herself all through the meal."

"What are we thinking of?" I said. "Do we want to spend Christmas with any of them?"

Pat was chortling now. "It might be fun."

"For us. I'm not sure about Martha."

"Don't be so protective of Martha," said Pat. "She can take care of herself."

I wasn't so sure, but I was delighted that I did not have to rescind the Christmas invitation.

It would be my first Christmas since 1954 without my buddy, Tom. For five years we'd spent the day together, wherever we were, whomever we were with, sharing the cooking, any strays invited, same as we had them for Thanksgivings. Tom was so certain I'd want to be alone with Pat, that he had decided to go to his family in Omaha.

The day after the night of Chianti, with a painful hangover, I drove into New Hope, since I wasn't in any condition to work. Pat had been up as usual at dawn and was typing away in her study. I began talking myself into Christmas, rationalizing that with a lot of people around I probably wouldn't drink a lot. I seemed to get into my cups much more enthusiastically when just Pat and I were drinking. I was beginning to realize that, partnered with Pat, I was becoming a bush-league lush, no pun intended. I couldn't remember a time in my life when I thought so much about how to protect myself against heavy drinking. I'd never been with a drinker before.

I was going to a silversmith in New Hope, to get a Christmas gift for the house. Pat always preferred a cloth napkin: breakfast, lunch, and dinner. I'd decided to give us good silver napkin rings, our initials on the front, and on the back of Pat's: *with love morning, noon and night. from MM to PH.*

I did some other Christmas shopping, and drove home listening to the news on the radio: Norman Mailer was declared legally sane and released from Bellevue Hospital in New York City, after he was arraigned on a charge of stabbing his wife.

When I got home, Pat called out from her office that Knox Burger at Gold Medal Books had phoned. He was the new editor, replacing Dick Carroll, a man I'd adored.

Not only were they taking *Something in the Shadows,* Knox said, they would do a reprint of my novel about three juvenile criminals, *The Twisted Ones.* The print order was for 400,000 copies. It had been the only paperback on the *New York Times'* list of Boucher's Best for 1959. I had been in between Margaret Millar and Mary O. Rank. Knox said he liked my latest and a letter would follow with minor suggestions for revision. That call from Knox made me approximately eight thousand dollars richer.

Pat always dressed in flannel pants, an ascot, and a blazer for dinner, but this evening she appeared in a black skirt with her blazer, and a white silk shirt. A red silk scarf at her neck. Stockings, pumps. She had her switchblade out; she was busy grooming the houseplants, as she talked.

"I thought you'd feel like celebrating," she said, "so let's go down to the Black Bass." It would never occur to Pat to shun the Black Bass because their dress code had kept us from enjoying a good meal not that long ago. Pat put a higher priority on comfort and convenience than on retaliation. I think it was also why she often left things unsaid: She didn't want her mind cluttered with bad feelings. She knew anything she brought up (like Martha's early-morning vociferation) would be endlessly defended by me, with my working it around somehow so that Pat was to blame for whatever we were discussing. She would not have made a good debater. I was a champion.

"How did you know Knox's news would be good?" I asked her. "You might have gotten dressed for nothing."

"They phone good news," she said. "They *write* bad news."

"How would you know? Have you ever gotten a rejection?"

"One," she said. "Harper Brothers didn't want to publish *The Price of Salt*. My agent told me, and then the letter from my editor came.... Go get dressed."

Gold Medal had taken less than two weeks to accept the book. That was one of the blessings of paperback writing. They moved fast. I missed Dick Carroll, who'd smoked a pack of Camels every night after work, downing scotches in the Algonquin's Blue Bar until cancer gathered him. He had adored women, and the novelist Rona Jaffe, who had worked for him at one time, had made him the hero of her first best-seller *The Best of Everything.*

Knox wasn't Dick. He was sarcastic at best, and rude most of the time, but I couldn't fault him when it came to giving me money. I was, at that point in my life, too naïve to realize the reason: my books sold.

Before we went out that night, Pat's black cat, Spider, came home dragging a dead rabbit.

"I'm sorry," Pat kept apologizing as she disengaged the late bunny from Spider's mouth. "He can't help it. It's his natural instinct."

"I know that," I said.

"But your cats don't kill rabbits, probably."

"Not yet."

"Why do you think that is?" she said.

"Because Spider's a natural killer. He's a Highsmith." It was supposed to be a joke.

"I knew that's what you were thinking," Pat said...and she was serious, her face solemn. Always ready for the blame. That part of her was an enigma to me.

Twenty

A few days before Christmas, Tom came from Princeton with gifts for us: caviar and brie and glasses for Irish coffee. I'd made his favorite, rib roast, for dinner.

While I was struggling to get everything ready (the Yorkshire pudding rising in the pan juices as I barely simmered the fresh spinach), Pat and Tom sat in the living room speaking German and drinking martinis.

Pat grabbed at any opportunity to speak German, and Tom told me he could not believe how perfect her accent was considering she was self-taught and seldom spoke it.

Tom really liked Pat, one of the few friends I had who did. More felt that she had spirited me away from New York, and that the next destination would be Europe.

That night, at dinner, Pat asked Tom why he had chosen to write his novel in Princeton—why not in France or Italy, since he was so good at languages, and since art history was his field?

"I think I wanted to be near Dr. Meaker," he said. His psychiatrist friends had nicknamed me "Doctor" because I had picked up Martha's strange speech pattern. "She's the one who got me thinking about writing. Did you know she sold my first short story?"

When I was my own literary agent, and Tom's neighbor, he had written two slick magazine stories under the name Whit Cameron. ("Witless," he'd dubbed himself.) I'd sold them both to a magazine published in Canada, called *Extension*. It was a Canadian version of *McCall's* or

Redbook, each issue featuring a love story.

Tom's first sale was called "Remember, Remember." It was about a man taking his bride to see the temples of Paestum, in southern Italy, where he had been in World War II.

"I've been there," Pat said. "I remember Paestum well."

"So does Witless Cameron," Tom laughed. "I went there when I was an ensign in the Navy. This army captain took me—a doctor, a real number. My first real love."

"Wouldn't it be nice if our truths didn't have to be disguised?" Pat said. "That's why I don't write about myself."

"Don't you think you were a bit like David in *This Sweet Sickness?*" I said.

"I could create him, but I could never be him," she answered.

"But part of you knew all about the jealousy that was driving him. A big part of you, I would think."

"What about you, Tom?" she changed the subject.

"I just told you. I put the captain in a skirt with a purse and we went back to Paestum."

"Maybe I do use a lot of myself," said Pat. "But I'd rather not think about it, for the same reason I don't believe writers should be psychoanalyzed. Leave the unconscious mind unconscious."

"Speaking of unconscious," said Tom, "I'd better go before I can't drive."

And so the Christmas holidays began with entertaining my next-to-oldest friend, Tom, and ended with my oldest friend, Martha, wishing she'd never left New York.

Even though it was not obligatory, we decided to dress for dinner at the Porters. Pat wore a red velvet two-piece suit, and I put on my gray cashmere. Martha never wore pants, anyway, but she, too, was in a red dress, to get into the spirit of things. Of course, that included a round of martinis before we left the house. Even I had one, which I sipped very slowly, while Pat and Martha finished off the residue in the small glass pitcher Pat kept in the refrigerator. It was then that Martha presented us with a Piranesi print, a combination housewarming/Christmas gift. We gave her one of the aprons Pat had fashioned out of ancient flour sacks we'd found in the barn. Across them she'd stitched "G I N." Pat had made several for her friends, and I got her to give me one for Kit.

Pat and I had decided to save our gifts for each other until New Year's Day.

Over the hills and through the woods we went, to an old-fashioned two-story house with four chimneys and white shutters. It was a few miles past Point Pleasant, near Betty and Al's.

Bud Porter wore monogrammed carpet slippers, a black blazer with gold buttons, and a white turtleneck sweater that kept his double chin raised. Big, round black-framed glasses, and perfect white teeth Pat said later were false. He was short and plump.

He greeted us, and strutted around getting our coats, finding out what we wanted to drink (he had made some ghastly eggnog that tasted more of egg yolk than brandy) and explaining that Hedda was with her dogs. She would join us soon.

It was a draughty old house filled with antiques, a cuckoo clock sounding off in another room, books everywhere, and little light coming in through windows with heavy curtains.

"A doctor of what?" Bud asked Martha. I had introduced her as Dr. Wolfenstein, forgetting she didn't like that. She said in Europe they addressed Ph.D.'s as "Doctor," but not in America.

"I received my doctorate in psychology," Martha answered Bud.

"So you're not an M.D.?"

"No."

"I didn't think you were an M.D.," he said cryptically. Then turning to me, the second guest he did not know, he said, "And you write these lurid paperback books, hmmm?"

"Yes," I said.

"They're no more lurid than my books," Pat said.

Betty and Al arrived at that point. We had had just enough of Bud Porter to grasp the fact he liked to find an Achilles' heel as quickly as possible.

The martinis flowed and there were smiles and small talk, and everyone began looking around…but there were no hors d'oeuvres. We had been told by Betty and Al that Bud did all the cooking, while Hedda did hors d'oeuvres and dessert.

We had eaten large breakfasts at eleven that morning, but it was now near five.

Pat seemed to be enjoying herself talking with Al. He would solve all her problems with carpentry: She was making bookcases for her study. She was a good carpenter and so was he.

Martha and Betty were admiring, or pretending to, a lamp Bud said he'd found at a road sale. It had a silk fringe, and a cameo-cut swan on its gold iridescent shade, a white marble base that supported a cast-gilt metal swan.

I remembered Pat's remarking that he collected antique furniture when he wasn't in New York picking up runaway boys in Times Square.

Just as we were all resigned to the fact we either had to stop drinking, or let go and let booze, Hedda Porter appeared.

She looked like a poor thing: circles under her eyes, little makeup, an osteoporotic posture complete with small hump, this thin tiny woman with one lame leg. We were told later she'd sprained an ankle tripping over her dogs. She had twenty-five basenjis. She wore a green sweater, a red skirt, and old brown sensible shoes. But: she was carrying a plate of hors d'oeuvres, with a decorative sprig of holly on the side. They were some kind of warm cheese on round crackers that looked like Ritz.

"At last!" Bud Porter said.

He grabbed a cracker before anyone else did. Hedda tried to reprimand him with a dirty look, but he didn't meet her eyes.

People were calling out "Merry Christmas, Hedda" and she was nodding and trying to look pleasant, getting herself some punch before Al stepped in and said, "Let me do that."

Bud Porter had a booming voice, like someone who had trained to be an announcer. Nobody could miss his remark as he held a cracker in front of him for inspection.

"This tastes just like semen!" he said.

Silence. Hedda's face went red. I could see Martha scowling.

Then Pat spoke up. She looked across the room at Bud and said, "You're the only one in the room who would know."

Laughter, but not loud laughter. Embarrassed laughter.

Bud set his drink down then and said, "I'd better go see about my goose."

Pat couldn't stop. "Your goose is cooked," she said. She was at her silliest then, high and more amused by her own remarks than anyone else seemed to be. I thought she was funny, too, but I could feel the tension in the room, the protectiveness toward Hedda, who looked nonplussed.

Somehow we got through Christmas dinner, with Martha making sure afterward that Pat did not drive. Martha drove. She said somewhat pointedly, "I never feel like drinking when I'm around people who aren't amusing."

Pat was admittedly exhausted, and gladly went upstairs to bed.

Martha said she never should have come, that even if the evening had been a pleasant one, she was too sadly reminded of other holiday times with Nathan and their friends.

I said I was sorry the people probably weren't that interesting to her, but we hadn't yet had a chance to make friends. We depended on Betty and Al.

"They were all right," Martha shrugged.

"They're very old friends of Pat. They helped us find this house."

"That Hedda," Martha said. "What a self-absorbed neurotic!"

"But look what she has to put up with—Bud."

"I hate to say people deserve each other because I don't want to believe I deserve Nathan now."

We sat drinking and talking together as we always had. The next morning Martha asked me to get her on an earlier train than she'd intended taking.

"What did she make of the Porters?" Pat asked that night.

"Oddly enough, it was Hedda she found hard to take, not Bud."

"Yes," Pat said. "He's just a fool, but Hedda's anger smolders. She wants you to feel her suffering."

"I don't see that at all. Hedda? She's just a sad sack."

"Those dogs she breeds can't bark. They're like her."

One of the differences between us was that Pat seemed to understand the intricacies of people's minds intuitively, while I read Freud, Stekel, Reik, to better understand crazy ways.

We cooked and knitted the same way. Pat took what was in the refrigerator and cupboard, a little of this, and a little of that and *pffft*—a perfect meal. I read cookbooks. Pat never learned how to knit: She just understood what to do. I had some lessons. When we knitted a long scarf together, her rows were neat and tight. Mine were loose and loopy, for I was too intent on manipulating the needles. It was similar to my failure to learn shorthand: I tried to draw the letters.

Three months after that Christmas, Bud Porter became very ill with stomach cancer. He wanted to move immediately to his hometown in Arizona, where his family was, his brothers and sisters nearby.

Hedda went with him, but before she left she personally chloroformed all twenty-five basenjis. She had to do it, she explained to Betty and Al. It would not have been fair to other breeders to simply give them away, and she did not have time to sell them.

Pat told me that after Hedda did that, she'd made notes for a short story about a woman whose sole diary entry for the day on which she'd killed every dog in her kennel was about a picnic she'd decided not to go on.

I have always thought that Hedda Porter was the inspiration for the character Edith of *Edith's Diary*. The novel's genre was neither murder nor suspense. The reader simply saw the woman lose her grip on reality.

Twenty-One

New Year's Eve we spent a lot of time hanging the Piranesi in just the right place, finally deciding that it belonged above Pat's piano in the living room. Pat cooked a pork roast with sauerkraut and boiled potatoes, and made fresh applesauce. We began *The Beast in the Jungle,* by Henry James, reading a chapter or two aloud before we went to bed. We were still awake when we heard whistles blowing in the distance, probably from the New Hope Fire Department. Pat went downstairs and brought up two glasses of Lillet for an impromptu toast. She laughed, remembering a letter of Louisa May Alcott in which she resolved "to take Fate by the throat and make a living out of her!" Pat said that would be her New Year's Resolution. "I don't care how long Joan Kahn takes to get around to me. I'm halfway through something new!" Kahn was her editor at Harper Brothers.

A few days later, Pat came into the kitchen chuckling while I was eating breakfast, saying she'd heard on the radio that the world's largest strike was over. The Barber's Assistants of Copenhagen, Denmark, had gone back to work after thirty-three years! It was the kind of silly humor she relished. That was the moment the phone rang.

It was Ann Carson, whom I had never met. She was Pat's agent.

I was delighted because I believed we were finally going to have news that *Janus* had sold. Pat was restless, I knew. Even though she was back on schedule, working every day, she'd remarked that she was trying to write short stories but she wasn't sure they were good. She had also begun having cocktails about a half hour earlier than usual at night.

I was about to go up to my study when I heard Pat say sharply, "Does that mean she doesn't want it?"

I stopped at the top of the stairs and listened.

"She *doesn't?*... What about a rewrite? Did she have suggestions for a rewrite?"

Pat listened to her agent for a while and finally said, "I didn't think it was my best, but I never thought it was that bad."

Then, "All right. Thanks, Ann. I know you did all you could do. You always have."

I hurried back downstairs to be with her. She gave a little shrug and a half smile. "You heard, hmmm? Is it really that bad?"

"No, it isn't. Another editor will like it."

She went into her office and brought back her coffee. We sat on the couch going over the stupid ground a writer sifts through once rejected, looking for an answer. Our cats had a way of gathering in the room where we were either celebrating something or suffering through it. My five Siamese and Lovelove, the Persian, settled on chairs, the back of the couch, the top of the bookcase. Spider always stuck with Pat, curled up on her lap.

Pat said, "It was that title. Why did I insist on calling it *The Two Faces of Janus?* It's pretentious."

"She wouldn't reject a book just on its title, Pat." I didn't even know Joan Kahn, which Pat pointed out in the next breath. "You don't know what she's like, and I do. She doesn't suffer fools, as they say. She's really hard-nosed. The book was soft and confusing."

I kept telling her that someone else would see its value.

The truth was I agreed with Pat, although that was not the time to say so. After a book like *This Sweet Sickness,* and *A Game for the Living,* which had preceded *Sickness,* her *Janus* was fragile and not convincing. But surely she could fix it.

I had wondered, before we lived together, how honest we were going to be with each other concerning our writing. Would we change and discuss works in progress? Or would we leave ongoing work in our separate offices, Pat's downstairs and mine upstairs? No discussions until after publication? Then we could say what we wanted but we could never be accused of interfering with ongoing creativity. Those were our rules, or at least that was our conduct: I can't remember that we ever spelled it out, but we were fairly strict about sticking with that way of doing things.

But there was no rule that we couldn't agonize, and Pat had been agonizing about *Janus* both while she was writing it and after she'd finished.

When Joan Kahn called late that afternoon, all cat ears pointed at the sound of the phone, and Mr. Schwartz meowed his usual blunt complaint about any telephone call.

Pat motioned for me to stay, and I sat on the couch pushing the silver bracelet she'd given me for Christmas up and down my wrist. It was a simple cuff bracelet, coincidentally made by the same New Hope silversmith who had done our napkin rings. Inside the bracelet were three words from a German folksong Pat would sometimes sing softly at night in bed.

Ich bin din.

I am thine.

Du bist min, ich bin din:
des solt du gewis sin.

"Yes, Ann Carson told me you didn't like it," Pat was saying to her editor.

Pause.

"All right then, you didn't *understand* it. And she also said you were dead set against it, that you didn't see a way to fix it."

Spider was winding his way in and out of Pat's legs as she stood holding the phone. She sat down so that he could jump into her lap.

"I'm sorry," Pat finally said, a forlorn look on her face. "So long."

She hung up and looked at me, shaking her head, bewildered.

She told me, "The last thing Joan said was 'Where did you get that title?' Henry James called a short story 'The Two Faces,' but I didn't get it from him. She can't accuse me of that."

"Pat, she probably doesn't even know about the Henry James story."

"She knows *Janus* was a Roman deity. She said the name is a symbol for double-facedness and for war."

Selfishly, I was thinking that she had written most of the book while she was in Europe, last winter. She couldn't blame living in America. She had given it a breather, two or three months, and then polished it in New York, at the end of summer and as fall began.

"Is Ann going to send the book to other publishers?" I asked.

"After I have another look at it.... You don't think I should just put it away and forget it, do you?"

"Absolutely not. You've spent too much time on it."

"I'm going to invite Ann Carson to come out so we can discuss it. What do you think?"

"Yes. I'd like to meet her."

"And Sunny," said Pat.

"Who's Sunny?"

"She says it's her cousin," said Pat. "I once wrote a story about the back of their bathroom door. I called it 'The Back of Their Bathroom Door,' too. You'd go into the bathroom knowing nothing about them, really. Then you'd sit down on the toilet, and the only thing you could see was the back of the door. On one hook hung Ann's shimmering nightgown. On the other was a pair of men's pajamas—Sunny's."

Pat got up to mix another drink. "I never tried to sell the story. I didn't want Ann to read it."

Twenty-Two

It was a hard winter. Because we were far from schools and main roads, surrounded mainly by farmland, no plow trucks came with any regularity. Two, three days in a row I would be unable to get the *New York Times* from Doylestown. It was like being without coffee or milk. How did you begin a work day without it?

We could always improvise and make meals of pasta or beans, eggs or canned goods. Our furnace was in good shape, and evening meals were pleasant because Pat always managed to shovel a path to the wood pile so that we could have a fire.

But besides the *Times*, I looked forward to the daily mail. Certain periodicals like *Publishers Weekly*, *Life*, *Time*, and the *Saturday Review of Literature* were part of my routine, and of course the only way you communicated with family and friends was usually with the cooperation of the United States Post Office. Both Pat and I regularly phoned only family, as well as a very few close friends—and even then not often. It was too expensive.

So we were isolated, together twenty-four hours a day, and trying as hard as we could to stick to our routines. Both of us were good at that. Pat was rereading *Janus* with an idea to rewrite it, plus working on a short story, and I was studying the life of Wilhelm Stekel, the German psychoanalyst who was Freud's colleague, and who had committed suicide by swallowing aspirin. Thanks to the Gold Medal reprint, which I hadn't counted on, I could give time to my suicide book.

I wanted *Sudden Endings* to have every kind of professional, from doctor to novelist to poet to film star to government official, but still neither Pat nor I could think of the suicide of a classical composer or performer of any note, nor a major sports star.

Our evenings were full of book talk, and reading, but Friday nights we both liked watching *The Twilight Zone* at ten, followed by *Eyewitness to History*. Sometimes I watched things by myself, but these two shows we usually watched together.

Then one snowy night, when we had not left the house in a few days, Pat got a surprise call from a woman named Natica Waterbury. I don't remember where the call had come from, or even what Natica had wanted, but it started Pat on a long trip back, a trip fueled by alcohol, nostalgia for Paris, for other times, other places, and I think of it still as a beginning to losing something we had.

I had met Natica only once—not a real meeting, but a quick introduction in a crowded room. She was very tall and blond and sensual. Somebody said immediately after, "Do you know who she is? She's Jane Bowles's lover."

It was before I met Pat. At the time, in New York, friends were just beginning to talk of Paul Bowles's book *The Sheltering Sky*. We knew better his wife's novel *Two Serious Ladies*, and we also knew of their strange marriage, which was not just a front for a gay man and a lesbian, but a peculiar, involved dyad.

That night of Natica's call, Pat said, "I met Jane for the first time in Mexico, in Taxco. She was the writer. Paul wasn't, yet. He was a musician and an eccentric, right away you saw that, and he smelled of patchouli. She had this upturned nose, and a pretty face, a bob, and she was lame from polio. But it was Paul who impressed me. He was blond, bearded," and then with a gleam in her eye she added, "He loathed America."

She raved about Paul, how brilliant he was, and how sarcastic he could be without being heavy.

"And what about Natica?"

"She was one of those women you love even if you get nowhere. I knew her a little in New York, but then when I was in Paris, in 1950, she was there with Jane."

Pat stopped what she was saying, sipped some wine, and smiled.

"They stayed in this little hotel in the sixth arrondissement, on the same floor," she continued, "and we'd go to the rue Mabillon to eat and drink in this café. Everyone was in Paris then!"

All six cats had joined us. Spider was on Pat's lap, purring, not a usual sound from His Blackness.

Pat began talking about Truman Capote, Gore Vidal, and the ex-Follies show girl Peggy Fears. She spoke of Ned Rorem, and Janet Flanner, and Jean Cocteau.

It was a two-bottle night; we opened another wine as we talked at the narrow table in the kitchen. We talked until the fire was out, and it was past midnight, still snowing hard out.

Pat told me then that, reading *The Beast in the Jungle*, she had a premonition. (We had finished reading the novel a few nights before.) She said maybe it was about her, or maybe it was about a character she was going to put in a book.

"But remember Marcher's feeling that he believes he's going to have a most unusual experience, that he's really marked for this in his life, even though he doesn't know whether it will be a horrible one or beautiful one?"

"Yes."

"Well, what if someone has the same feeling?"

"Go on."

"It could even be a murder."

"I suppose so."

"One you were fated to commit."

She was playing with her switchblade, which she always used to do indoor gardening every night before dinner. I put my hand on hers. "You're making me nervous."

"Sorry...." She shook her head as though she was shaking a thought away, a "never mind," but I persisted.

I said, "Finish."

She put the knife in her blazer pocket.

"I feel that myself...or my character does. Whether it's me, or someone I create, I feel it. I know exactly what James meant, only..."

"Only what?"

"It's not going to happen *here*." She emphasized "here" with an angry sound. She even hit the table with her palm and Spider jumped down.

"Not in this house?"

"Not in this country," Pat said. "Whatever destiny is, whatever it means, it won't happen in America."

Twenty-Three

For Pat's birthday we had planned to go to New York. I had gotten tickets for Eugene Ionesco's *Rhinoceros*. After, I wanted to show her my favorite French restaurant, Tout Va Bien, way west in the 40s.

We were going in on the 18th of January and coming back on her actual birthday, the 19th. I was treating her to a night at the Plaza Hotel.

A weather report promised a major storm the night of the 18th, and we were afraid to leave the house unattended with the animals in it. There was no one we knew who would stay there, and we could not depend on someone to take care of things if this was one of Pennsylvania's punishing winter deliveries.

Pat said the only sensible thing to do was for me to see the play. She said it would be good for her to be alone, even if I couldn't get back for her birthday. It would be good for me to see Kit, and Martha and some of my other friends. She said that she was used to being alone and it had been a long time. The clincher was her admission that staying at the Plaza would mean nothing to her because she didn't particularly like luxury hotels or restaurants.

I had drinks with Martha at her apartment on Central Park West. She was working on a book about disaster. She said disaster victims all had the same reaction, whether they had lost their homes in a flood, or some members of their family in a fire—whatever. They always seemed to say the same thing: *We were lucky.*

"Do you miss New York at all?" she asked me.

"Now that I'm here, I do. When I'm there, I don't. I don't even think about it. I don't miss friends, because they can come out."

"And you can come in," Martha said flatly, as though that would be what I would be doing if I wanted to see her. I think she'd had her fill of my life in the country with Pat.

I took Kit to the play and then we went to Tout Va Bien, where Kit and I had our favorites: escargots first, then frog's legs provençales. The owner, whom everyone called Madame, walked from table to table, singing songs like "Non, Je Ne Regrette Rien," entertaining the French sailors who were regulars. Afterward, Kit and I went to some gay bars, including Chez Mia, in the Volney Hotel, which had put Mia Fabrizzio back in business. Mia often took over failed restaurants with a year or two left on the lease. Gay restaurants didn't last that long, anyway, once the police discovered who the clientele were. They would suggest the price needed for protection. If it was refused, they would raid the place with the excuse drug traffic was underway there.

It must have been a shock to the sedate East 60's Volney Hotel once they realized Mia's customers were mostly female. They could not be hookers since there were few men, yet the coat room girl in the hall was kept busy until three in the morning, catering to this exotic group, many in pants. The hotel residents who ate dinner in Chez Mia were too early for Mia's following, most of whom were drinkers, not diners.

By the time management realized Chez Mia catered to lesbians, there were only months left on the lease.

Later, we went downtown to the Gantry, in my old neighborhood on West 13th Street. This was a rare mixed bar of lesbians and gay men, a combination that seldom worked because it was too hard to keep heterosexuals out if men and women were seen going in. Gays required privacy. You never knew when someone from your office, the school you taught in, or one of your clients would stroll in, see you, and conjecture your scene by the crowd you were with, or by your intimate attitude at a table for two. In the '50s you could still be fired for being a homosexual, or lose your lease, your straight friends, your family—even in a big city like Manhattan, you were safer in the closet. The ones who were out often had nothing to lose, anyway.

There was a guarded feeling, always, out in the world. It was easier for Pat and me. Our work was never in jeopardy because of our sexual orientation, and our families already knew. But there were countless discomforts that seemed unnecessary. There was the fear Pat would grab my hand in a store, or on the street, and cause people to stare or laugh. There were the guests of the Ferreses who smiled at us across the table and inquired, "You two young women live together alone?" Pat replied, "We two young women live together together." There were our neighbors' grandchildren who now went inside when they saw our car about to pass their house. On and on. For all the acceptance in places like New Hope, where there were many male homosexuals, and at that time almost no lesbians, and for all the knowing approval, one was always annoyed that we needed it, that there were actually laws against our loving one another, and that not a single religion would support our relationship. The latter was okay with us—we weren't religious, but we knew lesbians and gay men who were, and felt the rejection.

So how good it felt to be back in gay society, to sit in a dark little club and through the smoke see women or men holding hands, dancing, and looking at one another with love.

I saved the money the Plaza would have cost and stayed with Kit in the little one-room apartment she'd always kept on Horatio Street. She told me she was deeply in love with a CBS film editor, who was French, blond, and beautiful, and they had found a place on West 11th Street.

"But you'll keep this place?"

She shook her head. "No, I'm sure this time."

Before I went back, I met Bernadette, and for the first time any residual guilt I might have felt because I'd dumped Kit for Pat, disappeared.

I told Kit, "We've both met our others, haven't we?"

One of the good things about lesbian life is that most often you become good friends with your ex, or exes. They are more like family to you than family, usually, and eventually all is forgiven, whatever happened in the breakup.

There was no snowstorm, and I was able to find flowers in Penn Station, to present to Pat at the train station in Trenton. She was standing there in her sheepskin coat with the long scarf we'd knitted wrapped around her neck.

She seemed genuinely glad to see me, pulling in on a side road en route home, so that we could kiss.

The next evening we watched the inauguration of the thirty-fifth president of the United States, John F.

Kennedy, also the youngest ever to serve, and the only Roman Catholic president.

I liked watching the pomp and circumstance. I have always been curious about the times I live in, something Pat and I didn't share when it came to America.

At Kennedy's famous counsel "Ask not what your country can do for you—ask what you can do for your country," Pat chose the moment to go in the kitchen and feed the cats. I always thought she did things like that to see if it would irk me, the same as she complained habitually about Americans and women as though she was neither one. But I'd grown used to her ways and not yet tired of them.

The snow we had been expecting arrived the same day it was announced on the news that Marilyn Monroe was divorcing Arthur Miller.

We discussed Miller that night, Pat convinced he would years hence be known mainly for creating Willy Loman, the salesman of *Death of a Salesman.*

" 'Attention must be paid,' wasn't that the line?" Pat said. "Well, it will be, but not to his life's work, not by most people...not to *The Crucible* or *A View from the Bridge.* He'll be remembered for Willy Loman. That one character will stick in people's minds."

We began to play a game, naming authors who'd be remembered that way. J. D. Salinger: Holden Caulfield. Sinclair Lewis: Babbitt. Flaubert: Emma Bovary.

The irony of Patricia Highsmith, creator of Tom Ripley, inventing this game couldn't be imagined then, for Ripley had not yet been thought of as a series character. Highsmith, if she was known for anything at that time, outside of her pseudonymous gay novel, *The Price of Salt*, was known for *Strangers on a Train*, although she would often gripe about Alfred Hitchcock's name always preceding the title.

When I said, "F. Scott Fitzgerald: Gatsby," Pat said she'd never read the book. "I always wanted to. I have it."

"Let's read it next, " I said.

"I'd like to."

I fell asleep thinking Herman Wouk: Queeg; Richard Sheridan: Mrs. Malaprop. From then on, in the middle of whatever, one would say, "Evan Connell: Mrs. Bridge," or "John Updike: Rabbitt." We never seemed to run out of names.

This little game of ours was the catalyst to another kind of game, one I was always wary of, the behind-your-back mischief that could be merely the smoke from an old fire, or the eternal flame. The next morning as Pat was shoveling out and bringing in wood—we would be without mail and newspapers for a day or so—I went to look for her copy of *The Great Gatsby*, so that we could begin reading at lunch. On storm days we often ate together during the day; we always liked to do some reading with coffee after a meal.

I seldom paid attention to Pat's desk, or anything in her office. We both respected each other's privacy. But there, sticking out of Pat's cahier, was an envelope with a New York postmark, one I had seen a few days ago, no return address, and at the time had wondered vaguely about it. But I had been rushing off to New York, and I probably wouldn't have questioned Pat anyway. She had a lot of friends in New York.

The Fitzgerald book had given me my chance to take a closer look.

It was a very thin envelope with a piece of white paper inside.

On it was a charcoal sketch of a naked Mary Ronin, standing at a drawing board, looking down at a picture of Pat, in profile, with a cigarette dangling from her lips…a characteristic pose. Above the drawing board was a calendar showing the lone date JANUARY 19. Pat's birthday.

That was all.

That was enough.

Twenty-Four

Suddenly I went into a Protect the Work mode, familiar since I first met Pat, and had to watch my drinking. But there is another way of being in that mode that has nothing to do with cutting down on booze, and that is keeping your mind free from unnecessary disturbances.

Don't start something you have to follow through on, if it is going to interfere with work.

Put off any likelihood of emotional upheaval until you have the time for it.

Forget Mary Ronin. Pat was living with me now. Pat never went into New York, never even took the car to New Hope or Doylestown, so what was there to make of a birthday card?

Since I had very little revision to do on *Something in the Shadows,* I was attempting to write three chapters of my suicide book, plus an outline. Pat had suggested that when her agent Ann Carson visited us, I might show it to her.

I had already finished a chapter called "The Bitter One," about Arshile Gorky. Hart Crane was next.

Still…the card with a naked Mary stayed on my mind. I remembered that night in the Grapevine, when I had first heard of Mary Ronin, Meg Terry quoting *Othello* in a warning to me: *"Trifles light as air / Are to the jealous confirmations strong / As proofs of holy writ."*

I had finished Phillip Horton's biography of Hart Crane, and *Exile's Return* by Malcolm Cowley. Pat had started a book she was not sure was working. There was no taker yet for her *Janus*.

The snows were heavy and there were several times we were housebound, when even the cats couldn't high-step their way out to mouse-hunt in the barn. We managed to get to Doylestown to see *The Misfits*, but more often than not we had long dinners with two bottles of wine while we read Fitzgerald.

One night while Pat was clearing the table and doing the dishes I went into her study again, to get *Gatsby*. For the first time I opened her cahier and read the last entry. I had never done anything like that before. What I saw made me weak in the knees, and the blood rise to my neck and face.

After all these years another bitch! When will I ever learn?

I went back, sat down at the table in front of the fire, and told Pat it was her turn to read. I was too filled with anger.

We were still somewhere near the beginning of *Gatsby* when the narrator was proclaiming that his own cardinal virtue was honesty.

I interrupted at this point and said, "Not one of my virtues, I guess."

Pat looked across at me. "What do you mean?"

"The question is: What do *you* mean 'after all these years another bitch'?"

"What are you talking about, sweetheart?"

"About when you'll ever learn not to get involved with another bitch," I said.

She just looked at me.

"Don't you remember writing that?"

"Where?"

Then I told her...everything. About finding Mary's drawing, and about sneaking a look in her cahier.

Pat pushed her chair back with an angry expression. "I'll be right back."

When she returned she had the cahier with her. Her eyes were narrowed. She turned on the ceiling light. "Look at this," she said.

She slapped the cahier down on the table.

I looked, and I repeated exactly what I'd seen.

Pat said, "Look carefully, my dear. You never could read my writing. That word is *h i t c h*. Hitch, as in a hitch in my new novel. I told you I was having trouble with it!"

I shook my head, embarrassed, humiliated. "I'm sorry."

"The birthday greeting was just that: no more."

"How did she get this address?"

"I sent her a Christmas card. Is there a law against that? You sent Kit one, didn't you? And God knows how many of your other lovers!"

"Okay," I said, "I am mortified."

"You should be," said Pat. "This jealousy of yours is almost pathological, you know. Plus it's supposed to mean that you're the weak link, not me. The jealous one is usually the one who strays."

"I'm not about to stray."

Pat wasn't smiling when she said, "I wouldn't care if you did if you can't promise me that's the last time you'll ever read my cahier."

"It is," I promised. "I'm so ashamed."

"I want to believe you," she said. "I don't want to have to lock up things."

She shrugged, got out two brandy glasses, and said, "Let's get past it."

"Thanks."

"Let's not read *Gatsby* anymore. It's so ordinary. I don't even know the point of it."

"I read it in college, anyway."

"What I'd like to do is find this story Truman Capote wrote about Jane Bowles. I think it's with my old magazines. I think it's in *Mademoiselle*. Carson McCullers' sister is the fiction editor there. I think she bought it from Truman. It has 'Eden' in the title. It's about how Jane could do these fantastic imitations of people. Helen Morgan was one. In the story she—"

"Don't tell me," I said.

"All right. I'll find it tomorrow.... Truman really liked Jane. She could speak Arabic, if you can believe that. She taught herself, the way I taught myself German. She had this Arab girlfriend. She'd get these letters from her. The page looked like chicken scratches. She'd look at the page and say, 'She misses me.'" Pat began to laugh. "These chicken scratches told her that!"

Then she began to talk again about being in Paris, about Libby Holman, the singer, and Montgomery Cliff...the hotel on the rue du Bac. She poured herself another brandy and drank it fast. She said there was a time in Paris when she thought she'd be a painter instead of a writer. She said she still played with that idea. Art gave her more satisfaction.

At some point in her musings I interrupted and said I thought we ought to go to bed. It was late. I got up.

Pat did, too. She caught my hand. "Can't we go down to the docks first? I'd love a short walk."

That scared me.

I wanted to be sure she wasn't kidding.

"Where are we, Pat?"

"Why, Marseille. Marseille."

Twenty-Five

When I went downstairs for breakfast the next morning, Pat was already in her study, as usual. I could hear her typing. Beside my glass of orange juice was a note.

> *Dear Marijane, my darling Marijane,*
>
> *I remember what happened, in case you think I was so blotto I wouldn't. I think it was talking about Europe that did it. I know it must have scared you. I remember you saying you were frightened. It will never happen again. Let's make a pact. You will never look in my cahier again and I will never drink that much. I know what brandy always does to me. I'll give it up. Please forgive me and have a productive day! If we can get out, shall we go to dinner and a movie? I love you. Pat.*

It was my idea that we should have more guests. I was too focused on Pat, and she drank more when there were just the two of us. So did I.

We had Kit and her new French lover for a weekend, and other friends. Even Martha gave it another try, and Tom Baird came from Princeton for the same night. Then, around the time President Kennedy ordered the implementation of the Peace Corps, Ann Carson and her "cousin," Sunny, came for a weekend.

Ann was a large, poised blond woman with a faint resemblance to the old movie star Eve Arden, a big, wry, smart Southerner. Sunny was short and boyish, and the reason I remember Kennedy had just launched the Peace Corps is that Sunny was talking about volunteering. For years she had been an editor on a highly successful "little literary" magazine, but she was currently out of a job. She had a southern accent, as Ann did not, and she would probably have been suspected of being a lesbian, as Ann would not be…except for the fact she lived with Sunny.

It was hard, in those days, for women who "didn't look it." It was even harder for good-looking women who didn't. Add ambition to this and you can appreciate that it wasn't easy for Ann Carson to function as a successful agent. She did, despite the whispers, innuendoes, and smirks. A classy and dignified woman, she did what so many did to survive: invented a few ex-husbands, invented the excuse she and Sunny were relatives and it wasn't that unusual in the South for two female cousins to live together in a big city. She kept her social life to a minimum. Sunny and she lived in Greenwich Village, low profile, not eating out a lot, never appearing in the gay bars, sticking with a small group of other professional gay women.

Many, many years later, after Sunny was dead, Ann would undergo a sea change. I will always remember arriving for lunch with her at her favorite place, Le Perigord on East 52nd Street in New York. She was there ahead of me, her face flushed, her smile wide, a fur hat tilted to one side on her head. I realized she was a little tipsy.

"I just came in from the country," she said. "I've fallen in love, Marijane, so in love."

"Who is she?"

"It's a he," she said, and she named a popular author, one of her clients.

"We just left each other and he ran alongside the train blowing kisses at me," she said.

She told me he had been pursuing her for over a year, begging her to marry him. He was about to divorce his wife. One day as Ann was dressing for work and listening to the radio, she heard "On a Clear Day" playing. She said she listened and she thought, Why not let myself love him and marry him?

They were married for over twenty years before he died.

But that was a future no one imagined in the '50s.

That weekend we went for long walks, Sunny trailing behind us, whittling, wearing a cap, looking for all the world like a boy. Ann consoled Pat, all the while saying honestly, as she always did state the facts, that she wasn't at all sure she could sell *Janus* without a lot of rewrite.

At dinner that night we all drank too much, and Ann along with Sunny sang us some old revival hymns.

Ann also looked at my *Sudden Ending* chapters. She said there should be more, and she said she was not sure there was enough "editorial excuse" for me to write a book about suicide.

"You're not an authority of any kind," she said.

"What about being just a journalist, reporting the facts?"

"You're not a journalist, though," she said.

"Not yet," Pat said, "but everyone has to start somewhere."

Ann said yes, somewhere. Magazines, newspapers— there has to be some backlist for a publisher to give a writer a contract.

I was discouraged when they left, and Pat was, too. We immediately went to bed to make ourselves feel better. That always worked with us. We never lost that. Pat held me in her arms and whispered, "After all these years another bitch." I said, "When will you ever learn?"

Sometimes it seemed we would never hold a grudge; we would never be small-minded. We would never be like others we knew.

"All that Peace Corps talk from Sunny," I said. "She was just trying to get Ann to react, same as if she was saying I intend to leave you, waiting for Ann to say *don't.*"

We always rehashed our times with other couples in that smug way lovers have before they find out they're no different.

That Monday afternoon when I went to work in my upstairs office, I put away *Sudden Endings.* I put *The Forrestal Diaries* back on the bookshelf. The Secretary of the Navy had been copying Sophocles' "Chorus from Ajax" *(Oh! When the pride of Graecia's noblest race / Wanders as now in darkness and disgrace)* right before he jumped to his death from the window of Bethesda Naval Hospital. Symbolically, he fell from a great height. A quote from Dr. Wilhelm Stekel (when he was ill with prostatic trouble and diabetes), himself a suicide, was written across my Forrestal file: *The choice of the manner of dying is in itself a significant tell-tale feature.*

Stekel had taken ordinary aspirin.

The material was so rich, but I would have to begin thinking about something new.

Pat was interested in the recent kidnapping of Eric Peugeot, age five, grandson of the French auto manufacturer Jean-Pierre Peugeot. A trio of suspects had been rounded up after the release of the victim and a payment of $100,000.

At least she seemed resilient, able to enthuse about a new idea. I wasn't so sure I was, since I'd had my heart set on the suicide book. Pat had said to go ahead and do it. I was a bit ahead financially. Why not take the chance? But I didn't know how I could do that without something fairly certain to follow it. The freelancer's fear is not only "Can I sell this?" but "How can I live while I wait for this to be sold?"

I usually opened my mail before dinner, since it arrived in the late afternoon. Pat had her first martini then, while I drank coffee and looked at the New York papers I'd brought from Doylestown in the morning.

Pat's martini was imbibed as she strolled about with her switchblade open, tending to plants and listening to the classical radio station from Philadelphia.

I had received an invitation from Lorraine Hansberry to attend a screening of *A Raisin in the Sun*, starring Sydney Poitier. It would be in late March. I could bring a guest.

I asked Pat if she wanted to go and she gave back the strange answer, "Not at all."

"Why not at all?"

"I'm just not interested. You go."

"I will, but why are you so adamant?"

"I know the plot. Colored person thwarted, then colored person triumphant. It's not my concern."

"Okay. I'll probably go."

"I have other things on my mind. You ought to realize that."

"Anything I don't know about?"

"Maybe," she said.

She was walking around with this switchblade and her eyes narrowed and I said, "Put the knife away and tell me about it."

"You think you're funny, always mentioning the knife. I would never hurt anybody."

"I never said you would."

She flipped the button on the knife and put it away with a great show.

"Now do you feel safer?" she said.

I had an idea she'd had more than one martini, and as she went into the kitchen to make another, I figured it would probably be her third. She had that defended attitude she sometimes affected when she was high and upset.

I remember Ann Carson telling me that it wasn't just the rejection of *Janus* bothering Pat, it was breaking ties with Harper Brothers. She had had to do it once before, when they rejected *The Price of Salt*, suggesting that she stick to suspense. After that, she did, and she felt berthed with Harper Brothers, and with her editor, Joan Kahn.

She came back carrying her martini and she sat in the living room. She rarely joined me before dinner. I put the *Times* down and asked her if something was troubling her.

"I'm afraid it would be trouble to you."

"What would be?"

"If I did the research required to write the kidnapping case."

"The Peugeot case?"

"Exactly. I ought to go there."

"Pat, you're thinking of writing a novel, aren't you?" I couldn't believe she was pulling this.

"I should still do some research."

I looked at her for a minute, but she didn't react to what must have been written all over my face. She just shrugged as though there was nothing she could do about it.

"I wouldn't go with you," I said.

"Then I wouldn't go," she said.

"Whatever I do next, it won't help me to go to France…. And we had an agreement, remember? We'd try living here."

"I'm talking about a vacation," Pat said.

"I don't need one, but if you have to do it, do it."

"Not without you," she repeated. "We're a couple."

I tried to laugh it off. "Which one of the couple is making dinner tonight?"

She smiled. "Moi. I'm making us French omelets, salad, and we still have some French bread."

I said it sounded good, and I thought we could get beyond the idea of a French trip, but in silly ways, and then just in drunken talk Pat stuck with it. When she drank too much she liked to recall a part in Victor Hugo's *Les Misérables*, where the four inscriptions on wine goblets exemplified the four stages of drunkenness: monkey wine (lively), lion wine (irritated), sheep wine (stupefied), and swine wine (brutalized). She'd say, as she said that night clearing the table, "I'm into the fourth goblet."

I left her downstairs after I did the dishes and went upstairs to watch television. I wondered if she would really be any different in Europe, if she would drink less, write better, be happier. I remembered her mother telling me Pat was always restless, wanting to be somewhere else. Even though I knew in my heart that a trip there, or a move there, would not be a panacea, Pat always made me feel that I was holding her back.

Twenty-Six

One morning when I came down for breakfast, Pat wasn't in her study, as usual. She asked me to come outdoors for a moment. The sun was shining, and she pointed out the maple buds, the crocuses opening, and a cardinal whistling in our apple tree, his wife hopping about under it.

I was surprised at her good mood so early in the day. She said she'd found the story Capote had written about Jane Bowles. It was in her magazine pile, in a *Mademoiselle*. I would have a real treat that night at dinner. We'd read it together.

She hurried inside to squeeze us both some juice, while I was loading the car with laundry and books to take back to the library. When she handed me the glass, she took the other with her into her study.

Mine was strong with vodka.

I went back and knocked on her door.

"I think this is yours," I said.

She knew already she'd accidentally switched our glasses. She had her sheepish look, and monosyllabic tone, handing me her glass. She said, "Right. This is yours. I have a cold coming."

I set down the screwdriver and said, "I hope this helps."

In a way, it did help, for at least I understood the change in her I'd been noticing. Not just that morning's cheerfulness, either. I thought about it as I drove to do our errands. She was doing considerably more physical work in the late morning, carpentry and yard care and gardening usually left to afternoon. In the afternoon, she was sketching: the woods, the house, the animals. Pat was always lively when she was drinking. Sometimes after dinner, and an evening of heavy drinking, she would set up the ironing board and iron the white shirts she always wore. She did a good job, too.

But now she was apparently drinking all day, beginning with breakfast. By evening she was sullen, quiet, looking most unhappy when she appeared for dinner in the usual shined shoes, pressed trousers, blazer, white shirt, and ascot. That explained her new habit of reading at dinner, not aloud, but to herself. A book in German, most often.

When I returned to the house, I did my daily stint: the beginning of a suspense book with a fairly familiar plot. It was a lot like *Something in the Shadows,* two men interacting again. Pat would say, "So what? It's your theme. Sharpen it, take advantage of what you know from experience." But I knew it was my familiar hangover from the book just finished. I would be better off writing something completely different, and again I regretted that I couldn't do *Sudden Endings.* Ann Carson had convinced me it would be a hard sell, likely an impossible one.

I persisted with the suspense, wanting to feel I could control something besides the cats…and even then, they *were* cats. One, the lilac point Siamese named Peter Lewis, "Petey," who was Pat's favorite, insisted on looking out every door on days it rained, running from one to the other to the other, on the off chance that outside one it wouldn't be wet; it might even be sunny.

My confrontations with Pat were always after dinner. I saw to that. I'd grown up in a family where my mother waited for everyone to sit at the table, and then proceeded to tell my quick-tempered, work-stressed father everything we kids had done wrong that day. My brother had been playing in our new Lincoln Zephyr, released the brake, and it had rolled down the hill, smashing into the garage door. I had been looking in neighbors' windows at night with my club Spy Girls, and there were complaints. On and on until one of us kids would end up in the cellar being strapped with a length of rope.

So no dinner scenes.

But Pat and I did linger at the table by the fire, and apparently she had forgotten that morning's idea to read the story Capote had written about Jane Bowles. That was just as well with me. I didn't think I was up to another night of Paris remembrances. Besides, there was something important to talk about.

I said, "Why are you drinking in the daytime, Pat?"

A bit of a silence. Then she said, "I can't work."

"I'm having trouble, too."

"We need a change of scenery. There's nothing wrong with us, but we need to be stimulated."

I said, "There's an old saying that an ass who goes traveling doesn't come back a horse."

One word followed another. She remembered the night in Fire Island when I'd accused her of liking to be in Europe because she could always use her unfamiliarity with the language as a way of avoiding serious conversation. Did I consider a discussion of cocksucking with my friend Dr. Wolfenstein serious conversation? I accused her of envying Martha, and I said Martha was wise to her, too, because she'd read the French interview where Pat had said her favorite writers were Jouhandeau and Musil. Writers she'd never even read! Pat said the last person whose favorable opinion she'd seek would be Martha, who was not even a medical doctor. Yet she practices analysis!

I lashed out at her about blaming where she was for what she couldn't do. All of our frustrations and petty little complaints about each other were maximized. She was playing with her switchblade, sticking the point into the table, letting it quiver, then repeating the action, with a threatening glance at me that was silly and irritating. Before we were finished, largely due to my hot temper, and my fierce fear of losing her, I said she should move out. I thought that would frighten her, show her just how serious I was. I said, or screamed—I noticed the cats running from the hearth—"Get an apartment somewhere! Go into New Hope where there are people, and where you don't need a car! Then make your plans to go to Europe, or wherever it is you want to go! Please go! Please stop blaming me because you can't go!"

Pat replied, "Good idea."

She chose to sleep in the Rose Room that night. When I awakened in the morning, she was already on the downstairs phone calling about apartments to rent in New Hope.

There was no orange juice in the usual place on the table, and I left without breakfast, off to the library in Doylestown.

When I returned, Pat was packing.

She told me she had found an apartment that had a month-to-month lease, perfect for her while she decided when she could go to Europe. The apartment was mostly unfurnished, only a bed and a table, so would it be all right with me if she took her furniture?

"Fine."

"I'll leave anything you need. Maybe you need the long dining table in front of the kitchen fireplace."

"I have a table," I said, "and that's yours."

"Would you mind if I left Spider here for now?" she said. "There's no way for him to go out where I'll be."

"Please leave him," I said. "I'll take him if he can't travel with you, too."

She had actually called Move Away and made an appointment for the next afternoon.

I decided to go to Tom's for overnight. I couldn't bear the thought of having dinner there, of having to talk to her or not talk to her. I asked her if there was anything she needed before I left for Princeton. She mumbled that there wasn't, and I took off.

Tom said, "You know, if you really love her you should go back after dinner. I'll drive you so you don't have to worry about drinking and driving."

Tom had recently heard that Pennsylvania was very hard on drivers who were intoxicated. Someone high in the government had lost a child because of a drunken driver. The last few times Tom had come to dinner he had watched his drinks very carefully.

"You have a reason to drink tonight," he said. "I don't, and I don't mind taking you back."

"That would be a pretty scene. You taking drunken me back to drunken Pat."

"Then let's go out to dinner. You follow me to the Black Bass. We'll just have wine with dinner and then you're almost home."

I said I didn't want to go back.

I said this was going to happen sooner or later, so let it be sooner.

I stayed overnight, slept late, and enjoyed a sumptuous brunch Tom made for me.

When I got back to Old Ferry Road, the movers were carrying out Pat's furniture.

She was sitting at the long table in the kitchen, sorting through our silverware, making a point of putting the silver napkin ring I'd bought her and had engraved, with my things.

"I put the cats up in your study," she said. "Moving makes them nervous." She looked up at me. "It makes me nervous, too."

She was drinking a Heineken.

"Is there another beer in the refrigerator?" I asked.

She got up and got one for me while I took my coat off.

Soon Pat was making bullshots of the Heinekens with a bottle of Jack Daniel's. As we drank them, Pat's desk and chairs and bed went past us. We spoke calmly, Pat asking if it was okay for her to get her mail in our box until she knew exactly what she would do, if she would stay in Pennsylvania or not. She was saying that she'd prefer not to tell her mother she had moved, if her mother should call. She would prefer, she said, to tell her mother and friends in her own time.... Would I be all right out here in the country by myself? Would I be lonely? Her long fingers had reached across to stroke the fur on my gloves, lying between us on the table.

I finally said, "I can't believe this is happening."

"I can't, either," she said. "Es est ein traum."

"Meaning?"

"It's a dream. How could this be real? The German word for *dream* is where we got the word *trauma*. It's like a trauma."

"Worse," I said.

She looked at me across the table with just the slightest sign of a smile tipping her lips. She said in a low voice, "Shall we get past it?"

"Oh, yes! But we've got to stop the movers."

"I'll handle it," she said.

Twenty-Seven

Even though we had stopped the move and her things were back in the house, there was now an out: the half-furnished apartment in New Hope.

Pat had paid $300 rent through April.

Occasionally she would take the car into New Hope to visit her old acquaintance who, with her husband, ran an art gallery there. She had always avoided the woman and the town, in the past, saying she found them both boring. I think Pat had decided that it would be good for our relationship if she left the house now and then, and so once a week she'd go to New Hope.

In the summer months, New Hope was filled with antique hunters, buses of ladies and seniors attending the Bucks County Playhouse, a few art galleries, and many small restaurants.

The other months of the year, the town belonged to the locals again, few of whom were young, some of whom were old and male and gay.

Pat's acquaintance had kids, and Pat would return home complaining about them, saying how different American children were from French and Italian kids who respected their elders and weren't always featured.

Pat was away when her mother called one afternoon.

"I heard she got ditched again," said Mary Highsmith, not long into the conversation. "I warned her about it."

How had *she* heard? Pat had told me she didn't want her to know anything about our fight, the house in New Hope, her wish to go to Europe.

"What do you mean, Mrs. Highsmith?"

"Thank you for calling me that, though you have my permission to call me Mary. Very few of Pat's girlfriends have called me Mrs. Highsmith."

"What do you mean she was ditched?"

"By that tyrannical editor of hers, that Jewess, Joan Kahn. That's thrown her for a loop! She never learns."

"I think it's severing her relationship with Harper Brothers that bothers her."

"Don't kid yourself, Marijane. This is an old, familiar pattern. Pat gets these fixations on older women she puts on a pedestal and then they turn her away."

"But Joan's her editor. It's business."

"Oh, listen, I heard all about Joan Joan Joan the same as I heard all about Rosalind Rosalind Rosalind, and Lynn Lynn Lynn, and Doris Doris Doris and Lil Lil Lil, and you heard that Ellen Ellen Ellen got married, didn't you? How's that for rejection?"

"No, I think you're mistaken about Joan Kahn. Pat respects her, of course, and she's disappointed—"

Mrs. Highsmith cut me off. "Don't you see? It's another case of being swayed by a woman older than herself who will prove to turn against her…. I thought you'd get that. Pat says you're a writer, too, and smart."

"Have you given this fix on it to Pat?"

"She never wants to hear my opinions."

"But you told her?"

"Of course I told her. She said I didn't understand publishing. I only made my living for years and years as a magazine illustrator with all the top magazines, and then an illustrator of children's books, and I don't know publishing!"

It was her nickel, so the conversation went on for a while, and I saw how complicated the mother/daughter relationship was, particularly at the end of our talk.

"Well, it's been nice speaking with you, Marijane, and I hope you and Pat can get past the troubles you've been having."

"I hope so, too," I said, amazed that Pat had told her. I hadn't mentioned a word about it. "Getting past" was so much Pat's phrase.

"If you two move to Europe, you'll find she's no different there about wanting to go someplace else. When I was with her in Paris, she wanted to go to London, and in London she wanted to go to Rome. She's restless by nature. She always has been."

"Okay," I said. "I'll keep that in mind."

"Tell her she doesn't have to call back. I just wanted to be sure she was all right, and you two were still together."

I was accustomed to the idea, by then, that Pat was not a "spiller." That was my own name for myself. Kit used to say that no thought went unspoken. One of my favorite creations, a young man named Adam Blessing (*The Damnation of Adam Blessing*), could not count on himself to keep from blurting out his thoughts, his flaws, whatever came to mind, usually to his own embarrassment or disadvantage.

This was not Pat. I had never imagined her confiding in her mother, to such an extent. Pat's usual posture concerning Mary Highsmith was a very put-upon one. Her mother was her cross to bear.... Still, it wasn't completely unimaginable that Pat felt close to her mother, when I thought about it. There were the two books she had dedicated to her mother. All her women except me seemed to have met her mother, and Pat had mentioned to me that Mary Highsmith would probably "descend on us" sometime in the summer.

Of course this phone conversation became grist for the mill in all the succeeding arguments between Pat and me. Once we had called Move Away, we began the process of emotionally moving away, quarrels erupting whenever we were together. I accused her of being devious and mendacious, of crying on her mother's shoulder, then turning around and blaming her mother for trying to run her life. She said her mother was the devious and mendacious one, that she had a way of getting things out of her. "And don't tell me she doesn't get things out of you, too!" Pat said. She wouldn't hear my denials.

She was close to tears by then. She said, "Even before you laid eyes on me the first time, you imagined what I was like. When I wasn't like that at all, when I was me and not your version of me, you couldn't stand it! There's no way I can win!"

She was right but I couldn't admit it.

There were many nights Pat would call a taxi to take her to New Hope, where she would sleep in her apartment. Next day we would argue again on the phone, rehash old business, waste endless hours calling and recalling each other, until I finally drove in and got her—or she came on her own, in a taxi, late at night, drunk and weeping.

Too humiliated to call Move Away a second time, we called a small Mennonite moving company near Doylestown, when we finally decided again that we had to live apart.... And once again, just as the move was very nearly completed, we stopped it. As soon as the movers put back all the furniture and were paid for their time, we were dropping our clothes even as the van rumbled up Old Ferry Road. That was the only part of our love affair that had not been nicked. Maybe it even became more as we became less.

We knew it was over. We couldn't work. We couldn't be civil for very long with each other. We began to eat alone. We slept in separate rooms. We mentioned that the only thing keeping us together was the shame of having to call men to move us who had already tried. There were not that many movers in the area.

Ever the gentleman, Pat still squeezed orange juice every morning for me. One morning there was a note beside the glass.

> *I found a moving company down past Doylestown. They will come next Wednesday when you go to see* A Raisin in the Sun. *I'll handle all the details and feed the cats before I leave. They'll be okay overnight. You plan to be back Thursday, right? This is the only way to get the job done, as heartsick as it makes me. I don't think of this as a total split, but as time for us to think about what we can do with this love of ours. Pat.*

That was the week Foster Parents chose to publicize themselves in hometown newspapers of clients. A headline in the New Hope weekly announced: LOCAL WOMEN ADOPT KOREAN ORPHAN:

> *The writers Patricia Highsmith and Marijane Meaker have become foster parents, sponsoring a Korean orphan.* Etc., etc.

Twenty-Eight

Our mutual friend the artist Polly Cameron became a referee. I would telephone her in Palisades, New York, and pour out my troubles. I knew that Pat was calling her, too. I don't know what she told Pat, but she told me that I was expecting too much of Pat.

"First, you're making her live in this country when she hates it here," said Polly, "and second, you're not facing the fact that Pat was always a big drinker! She has Walking Drinks, and Talking Drinks, Cooking Drinks, and Doris even told me she had Planting Drinks when she had her garden here. You knew all that."

"I know. But I never knew she began drinking screwdrivers at seven in the morning."

"Marijane, from the moment you met her you complained about how much she drank, and how much you drank with her! Ask yourself: Does what you're saying about Pat have a familiar ring?"

"I think this is new. I think she's had trouble accepting Joan Kahn's rejection."

"If Joan had taken the book, she'd be celebrating too much. You still don't get it. She's a drinker, but she's not staggering down the Bowery from bar to bar. She works. Doesn't she work?"

"I can't live with someone who thinks we're in Marseille," I said.

"Pat's right about one thing," said Polly. "You made her up. Then you nagged her for not being the person you made up."

"We're both disappointed," I said.

"But she's not as disappointed as you are. She'd never heard of you before you met. She'd never read any of your books and wished she'd written them."

"And she doesn't even own a camera," I said.

"What's that got to do with anything?"

"Do you know how many rolls of film I went through when I first met her? I loved her looks. I really was overwhelmed by everything about her, you're right."

As good an arbitrator as Polly might have been, there was only one way to solve the dilemma of Patricia Highsmith and me. It took until late April to find the solution, a little over two years from the night I first saw her standing at the bar of L's.

My friend Tom Baird was celebrating his thirty-sixth birthday on April 22nd. I knew there were two things he loved best: my pot roast, and reading aloud his latest chapters of the novel he was writing. His birthday fell on a Saturday, so I asked him to come to dinner, and to bring chapters of *Triumphal Entry* with him. He brought his cocker spaniel, Alice, with him, too, and the cats hid upstairs while Tom and I and the dog settled by the fire in the kitchen, after dinner.

Since Tom was an art historian, his novel (published in 1962 by Harcourt Brace) was set in the art world, and the world of academia. He had brought four chapters with him, fifty-two pages in all. During dinner we talked about Pat, so much that my mind kept drifting from his book to Pat and me and our unsolvable situation.

Writers that we were, we wrote each other many letters, when we were not on the phone to each other.

A March 19th handwritten letter proclaimed: *I do love you and want you and want to spend my life with you—more than anything in the world, and by this I do mean anything. Last Monday I think we felt something that was quite different. I am sure I did. It was happiness and wisdom and a quality of love for you I had never felt before. Because we have been through so much, and because we still love each other.*

Three days later a long typewritten letter began:

> *To plunge in medias res, as I have just left you this morning, I should like to state clearly and without interruption that I do not blame you for last evening— that is, if I showed my drinks (two quick ones on a very empty stomach) I am to blame for showing them I grant you. But I also think you chose to make entirely too much out of my comment on* Rabbit Run, *that the break-up of that marriage ran through the book like a crevice—of the spirit—regardless of the man's statement that it was a second-rate thing to begin with. He so needed people that he went to his old basketball coach and then to a whore. It may be a dull statement. It was something I felt. I do not see why I have to be pounced on for it, unless you simply want to pounce. I think you do—and if it hadn't been this comment, it would have been another....*
>
> *You have a great deal to say about my drinking, much justified, some exaggerated. I shall improve in that direction. But I do not think it unreasonable of me to suggest you look into your own motivation, too, for blowing up storms over comparatively little. It could be*

that you never really liked me from the start, that you wanted to get to know me, really know me, for a very short while and then—finish. It could be that without any drinking at all on my part, you simply wouldn't like me as a person.

On and on we went. If we had not had such good horizontal rapport we could have been free of each other. The other bothersome thing was that we were stranded in this community of strangers. Neither of us had real friends to be with and help distract us from each other. And I think neither of us could believe that something that had seemed so right in the beginning, when we were madly in love, could so suddenly be shown to be a terrible, irredeemable mistake.

Tom had arrived that night when it was still light enough for him to admire the shadbush in blossom at the edge of the woods on our property. When he left it was dark and raining.

A few times Pat had surprised me late at night, arriving without calling. I decided I'd do the same. She had been nagging me to find some contour sheets that belonged to her and I finally had. I thought it would be funny to show up with the sheets, which I always mistakenly called "contact sheets." She'd tease me about it.

I put water on the fire, fed the cats, and took off. It was a little after eleven P.M.

What I hadn't counted on was the fog rolling in over the hills on the unlighted, winding back roads leading to New Hope. I almost turned around, but before I made the decision to go back home, I steered straight into a telephone pole.

I felt a tremendous jolt, and saw the windshield of my small English Ford smashed. Although I could tell that I was okay, my hand and arm were bleeding and I could not open the door on the driver's side. I could not get the car to move, either, forward or backward.

I wiggled across to the door on the passenger side and got it open. With some difficulty because my hand and arm hurt, I managed to climb out of the car, which was at a tilt.

There were no street lights, but the crash had made enough noise to alert the couple who owned the only house in view.

The woman stood in the doorway, while the man came to get me, carrying a flashlight. He looked the car over, shaking his head.

I held on to him as he led me back to his home. He was a big man, tall and sturdy. I told him I was on my way to a friend's, and he asked me who the friend was, and suggested we call Pat, because there was no way I could drive that car.

His name was Burton Brewster. He was balding, hair everywhere but on his head, with huge hands and feet— someone comfortable, you had the feeling, under cars, on the top of ladders and in sheds.

His wife was thin, long black hair, a white terrycloth robe over a white nightgown.

Before he introduced us, he asked me if he should call Patricia Highsmith. Could she come and get me? I said I didn't want to bother her. She would be angry with me for driving on such a night. I said I'd call a taxi and go home, and I told him where I lived.

He was in his forties, about twenty years older than she was. They were the kind of couple about whom, when you first met them, you wondered why she'd married him. Later on you knew she was probably lucky to have him.

"This is my missus, August," he said. "August, this is Marijane Meaker. I'm going back to her car and see if I can get it in our driveway."

"I don't want to trouble you," I said, foolishly.

He shook his head with a sorry smile. "I hate to leave your car in the ditch that way. We'll have to phone the police, too. It's the law when there's an accident." He wore jeans and slippers, with a T-shirt that read HOW DOES YOUR GARDEN GROW?

August had gone for a towel to wrap around my arm. "You'd better come with me so we can wash the blood away," she said. The scent she wore was familiar. I wasn't yet sure why. Her straight black hair spilled past her shoulders. "I don't know if the police will come here or not. Burr and I are good friends with them. We grew up out here. They might just take the report over the phone."

"Then I'll get a taxi."

"People call me Gus," she said, smiling. We were in a bathroom with pink and white tiles. Her eyes looked all over my face. She was a most unlikely Gus. She was feminine and flirtatious, even in that grim circumstance.

"People call me M. J."

"Is it Patricia Highsmith, the writer, Burr was talking about?"

"Yes. We shared a house up on Old Ferry until last month."

"Burr didn't even know who she was, but, see, I read a lot," she said.

I said, "So do I."

"I know Patricia Highsmith."

"So do I," I teased.

She gave me a look. "You know what I mean. I've read her."

We went about getting my arm and hand bandaged. I'd actually picked some small glass fragments from my fingers.

"Tell me about Patricia Highsmith," she said. "I saw *Strangers on a Train*. I loved it."

"Well, for one thing, in her book, Robert Walker was an architect, not a tennis player. It was Hitchcock's idea to make him a tennis player."

"I get it!"

"What do you get?"

"A tennis player is more effeminate! That would make their relationship more suspect."

"Yes." She'd surprised me with that. Hidden on the back roads of Bucks County, I wouldn't imagine she'd come from a rich local family, gone for a year to Bennington College in Vermont, and married the man who managed her father's nursery business.

"It's a good thing you weren't drinking," she said. "You wouldn't be able to drive in the state of Pennsylvania for two years."

Tom and I had drunk a bottle of wine with dinner, but that was all. I thought: Thank God Tom had brought his novel to read.

"What else about Patricia Highsmith?" Gus asked.

"Nothing else about her," I said.

"She's renting an apartment in a house Burr land-scaped.... What do *you* do?"

I was telling her about myself when Burr came inside to say there was no way he could move the car. He said that only a wrecker could move it.

"Call Ted Annan, Burr. See if he has to come here, or if Marijane can go over to the police tomorrow."

"I'll see," said Burr. "It's really coming down out there."

"Can you call me a taxi?" I asked him.

"I'll run you home. You say you're up on Old Ferry?"

"Yes, but you've done enough already."

"I'll get dressed," Gus said. "I'll take you home."

"My wife sees better in the dark. She's like a cat," Burr said.

"I really insist on taking a taxi," I said.

Gus laughed. "Nobody insists in my house but me."

Burr laughed, too. "That's right. She rules the roost."

(A month later, after a dinner there, he would walk me to my car and say gently, "Don't let her hurt you, Marijane.")

Burr phoned the police from the kitchen, while Gus changed into jeans and a sweater, sitting down to slide into a pair of sneakers. She was jabbering away, apologizing for the looks of the house, which looked fine to me, and announcing that she was still getting over the loss of her bulldog who had been twenty when he died. "I always thought I'd be a writer myself," she was telling me. "Of course everyone thought that at Bennington. Nobody was just going to be a wife."

"You're not just a wife," Burr was back. "You run the business, don't you?" He didn't wait for her to answer. He said the police took the information over the phone.

"Tomorrow I'll call Doylestown Ford to tow your car," he said. "I know them there."

"We know everyone," Gus said.

"Want me to drive with you while you take Marijane home?"

"What for?" she said.

"No reason," Burr shrugged. "But be careful, Gus."

We lived about ten minutes away from one another. Their house, like mine, and like so many in those farmlands, was isolated. There were no other lights at night. Their road was also not a usual, or direct, route into New Hope.

In the car Gus said, "You're going to need someone to help you shop and stuff, so it's a good thing you found us."

"I'll rent a car," I said. "I hate imposing on people."

"If you'd gone down Aquabogue, which is the real way into the village, you'd have caused a big commotion. There are a lot of houses."

"And telephone poles," I said.

"Exactly. But you found us. There must be some reason for that. That's the way I think, that there are hidden connections and hidden reasons. Do you think that way?"

"I'll tell you tomorrow," I said.

"When I drive you to get your rental car," she said.

Of course I knew Gus was right: There was a hidden connection and a reason. She would become the solution I was searching for, a way to free myself from Pat. I knew it as well as I knew the scent she wore while she had bandaged my arm in the bathroom: Celui, a perfume Lilo used to wear and put on Parrot Como. I knew that I had crash-landed into Gus's life to become a part of it, if only for a summer.

Epilogue

i

After twenty-seven years without a word from Pat, this letter was forwarded to me by the Authors Guild:

6671 Aurigeno
Ticino, Switzerland
18 October 1988

Dear Marijane,

I think you are living near the Hamptons, or you were. But surely the Authors Guild is a safer way of reaching you.

It occurred to me a couple of years ago (and I did nothing about it) that you might have a missing 3 pages from my family papers, which you were interested in—around 1960, in New York still. These are 33 to 36 (page numbers or nearly so). They were interesting because they were of Civil War years, and quoted passages from a couple of personal letters. You may well have returned them to me, and it is I who mislaid them. Before and after pages are all there—so you can imagine how I miss these.

Anyway, since you were always so orderly in your personal letter files and such, I thought it worthwhile to ask you about this. I'd be very happy if you had them and could return them. As I write this—am sitting on ancient pillow (which has not always been in use) with

center patch embroidered "Petey." You remember your
cat called Petey, no doubt! I do.

Wishing you good health, and all the best!
Pat

I was pleased to hear from her. I had no bad feelings
and I felt from her tone that she didn't, either. I knew nothing about her family papers. I wasn't aware there was such a
thing, nor could I figure out what she thought I would be
doing with them. I answered with a genial letter and a few
questions, signaling that I was glad to be back in touch, and
anticipating catching up with each other.

Pat was the only ex-lover I hadn't stayed good friends
with, probably because she was living in Europe. I have
always kept track of people, some who go as far back in my
life as elementary school. But Polly Cameron had lost
touch with Pat and there was no one else to tell me where
she was or with whom. I could have asked Ann, our mutual
agent, but I didn't. I think I felt deeply sad about the whole
episode. I refused to dwell on it. But I read every novel by
Pat that was published.

I was curious to learn how her life had turned out, and
for five years we wrote each other fairly regularly. I explained
that I had stopped writing mystery and suspense. I was now
writing novels for young adults. It was largely thanks to a
children's writer named Louise Fitzhugh *(Harriet the Spy)*,
who was my neighbor when I moved back to New York in
the '60s. She had pointed out that many of my suspense
protagonists were teenagers, and she thought the field might
be a new challenge. Because I've always loved the disguise
of a pseudonym—your only opportunity in life to name

yourself—once I sold a young adult novel to Harper/Collins, I made a new pen name from Meaker: M. E. Kerr.

Pat's letters were usually on hotel stationery (Hotel zum Storchen, for example) and the backs of announcements and invitations (Yaddo, inviting "friends and associates" to hear the composer, conductor, and flutist/teacher Otto Luening).

In the beginning we shared news of old friends: *Ellen B. Hill lives two villages away, in Cavigliano 6654, just "up Centovalli" some 2 kiloms. You remember when she visited us in Pennsylvania, with her new husband, Shep? That didn't last. I've rather parted company with her, which is sad, as she became 82 on 20 Jan.... Ellen adores scolding people for minor misdemeanors such as being 5 mins. late for a date because finding parking spot was difficult. Need I say more?*

Pat's letters were filled with complaints about her mother, and how much she had cost Pat. I'd tried to clarify for Pat how her mother could qualify for Medicaid, but the Texas relatives weren't interested. Pat wrote: *Mother went into the nursing home in 1974. We weren't even speaking when she could still speak. I paid most of her bills there. I never knew all those details you wrote me about Medicaid. It was too late by the time I found out I wasn't responsible for her bills, that Medicaid would pay them. Nobody in my family pointed that out to me. My cousin might not want to have the family connected with Medicaid. He might think it would look like we needed charity. Or maybe something fishy is going on with the checks I send. I wrote a story about it called "No End in Sight." I made myself a son instead of a daughter in this story, otherwise it's my father and stepfather. My mother lives on, a veg., at 95, an age no one in the family has ever reached before.*

In another letter she wrote: *When you make a lot of money you get suspicious. Did I tell you that Bloomsbury liked my latest Ripley so much they gave me an advance that in American money comes to about $115,000? I never got that much for a book. You know, in the U.S. no one really recognizes me, but in Europe I'm often recognized and treated like a celebrity.*

Pat mentioned her celebrity status often with surprise and pleasure, and just as often grumbled about reporters wanting to interview her, and photographers trying to photograph her.

I encouraged Pat to apply for Social Security, after she complained that she had nothing to show for all the money she paid as U.S. taxes. She had been misinformed by a European accountant that she did not qualify because she lived abroad. It was her due, after all, and she was successful in her efforts and inordinately pleased with the monthly check.

Neither of us mentioned the books we'd written immediately after our split. Pat's was called *The Cry of the Owl*, featuring Robert Forester and set in Pennsylvania. She often wrote from the male viewpoint, just as often interchangeable with her own. The females were familiar to anyone who knew Pat well. In this book, Forester had an ex-wife, Nickie, who was a chain-smoking, argumentative, unsuccessful artist. (When Pat and I lived together, she often declared that my anger at her about anything was dissatisfaction with myself, because at that time I had never been published in hardcover.) Nickie had many pseudonyms (as I do), in particular "Amat." She and Robert had been deeply in love, and then just as suddenly as it had begun, it had ended in her jealousy, her taunts and rages.

Ultimately, Nickie was knifed to death, for several pages at the end. That was Pat's adieu to me.

My book was called *Intimate Victims*. The hero was named Harvey Plangman, Plangman being Pat's real last name. Harvey was in no way like Pat. I probably just wanted to kill her off, too, so I chose Plangman for the victim's name. I also featured Gus in the book, renamed "Bunny," the Bucks County female who had helped me get over Pat.

The *New York Times* reviewer, Anthony Boucher, said, *Miss Packer's eye and ear for nice distinctions of culture and usage are as acute as those of John O'Hara and Nancy Mitford, and her two protagonists are impressive full-bodied characters.*

But to my embarrassment, James Sandoe, the *Herald Tribune* reviewer, began his criticism this way: *A decade ago Patricia Highsmith introduced us to a pair of strangers on a train whose chance meeting scarred them both indelibly. Now Vin Packer introduces us to a pair, the one a large-scale embezzler…the other a bootstrap johnny.*

Sandoe went on to say: *They do breathe and one follows their disparate, interwoven histories with fascination.*

But I never really recovered from the opening lines.

Both of us shared the same agent—at the time, Ann Carson. Both of us had been told about the other's book. I'm sure Ann couldn't resist sharing the Sandoe review with Highsmith, either.

Sandoe had once taken Pat to task in a review because she had dedicated her book to her cat, Spider.

Spider, according to a letter from Pat, had done all right for himself: *I couldn't take him to England with me because of the endless quarantine they impose on incoming pets. But*

Muriel Spark heard about this, met him and adored him, so he went to live in a villa in Rome.... After that, most of my cats were Siamese. You gave me a taste for them.

In many of Pat's letters there were pejorative remarks about Israel and the Jews. She had told me she refused to sell to Israel the rights to any of her books.

I knew, too, that her then latest book, *Ripley Under Water,* was dedicated to: *the dead and the dying among the Intifadeh and the Kurds, to those who fight oppression in whatever land, and stand up not only to be counted but to be shot.*

I thought of her vendetta with Israel as a displacement, that her real anger might have been at American publishers who she felt were largely Jewish, and unappreciative of her work. From what she wrote me about her life she had never been a part of any political group or movement.

She once sent a Xerox of the *Kirkus Review* for *Mermaids on the Golf Course.* After complaints about Highsmith's *morbid obsessions, suicidal urges, and considerable nastiness,* the reviewer had summed up: *As in some other Highsmith work, unconvincing American settings and characters add to the artificiality of several stories in this collection.*

Across the top, Highsmith had written: *M. M. Sample of Kirkus dishing. If this is East Coast Jews hitting back, I can be only flattered.*

Her letters ultimately took off after France, too, and England, on and on and on, as though it was her only way to vent once she began to withdraw from people, live alone, and call herself a recluse. She also called herself "The Famous Grouse," a little levity usually following one of her tirades.

Sometime in the early '90s Pat and I began talking about getting together. I told her frankly that she would have to be the traveler, that I knew she liked to travel, and I *didn't*.

Don't tell me you still resist Europe? she wrote. *I won't insist that you stay very long.*

Then she began to suggest dates when she could visit me. In the old self-deprecating way that was familiar, she would add things like *By this time, I don't blame you if you (mentally at least) say to hell with my visit.*

Or, *My idea is to come to NYC, stay about a week, go to Texas for a few days with my family, then see you (if convenient). I have no plans to see anyone else.*

As it turned out, the autumn of 1992, Pat went directly to New York for overnight, then to Weatherford, Texas, for three days, and on to East Hampton to visit me for three more.

ii

Late on a Tuesday afternoon, Pat arrived on my doorstep a little drunk, grinning shyly, carrying a gallon of Dewar's scotch.

I had sent Sean, one of my former students from the Ashawagh Hall Writer's Workshop, to meet her flight and bring her to East Hampton. He was still pursuing writing, but now he had his own limo service. He also had a great admiration for Patricia Highsmith.

Pat was in a trench coat, dark pants, a black V-neck sweater, her trademark white shirt, and a black and blue ascot. I had seen photographs of her, including London's 1968 *Tatler* cover, which was a gruesome close-up of her scowling, wrinkled face, puffy lips, angry eyes, and age marks. I had also watched a PBS interview with her lurking in and out of the shadows in a trench coat, a cigarette hanging from her mouth, her discomfort at escorting the cameras through her house in Switzerland evident in frowns and grimaces.

It took me a while to see the remembered young face in the old one. Still, she was nowhere near as unattractive as were most of the photographs I'd seen of her in magazines and newspapers. The shy eyes and the slanted grin were familiar. I recalled how handsome she was once.

She was still thin, but her shoulders were stooped, and she no longer walked with those sure, long steps.

I thought that Sean might enjoy a photograph of himself with her, and I snapped one of them together after she paid him.

We hugged hello when he left. I felt that we were both awkward, or perhaps only I was. We'd been together so long ago, for such a short while, and yet I remembered the feeling in the '50s, the first time she'd merely touched my arm with her hand. I'd felt a beginning with her immediately, and with it a strong physical vibe, an electricity running down my arm through my fingers. Later, she told me the Germans, who have a word for anything and everything, have a word for that, too: *fingerspitzengefühl.*

"You still always have your camera ready, ha?" she said.

"Do you mind? I'm near the end of a roll."

"Take all the pictures of me you want but I'd prefer not to be with the driver. He'll probably sell it."

I explained he was a member of my workshop and a fan of hers.

"That doesn't mean he won't sell it," she said. Then quickly changing the subject, losing her grumpy tone of voice, she cried out, "I'm starving! I could really use a drink, too! Where are your kitties? Here, kitties!"

She was chattering away. Nervously? I felt that was so.

My yellow hound dog was sitting in the hall regarding her solemnly, as he did strangers he wasn't certain how he felt about.

While I was getting out ice cubes and a glass she said, "You know, you don't get anything decent to eat on planes, anymore, even in first class. Remember the wonderful ham sandwiches they used to serve?"

"I never went first class, so I don't remember them."

"They were great, big thick ham sandwiches. Not anymore!"

She sounded as though she knew the reason so I asked, "Why?"

She put one finger up to her face and pantomimed a hooked nose.

"The yids had it stopped, I suppose!" she said.

Then she chortled—she was one of the few people I know whose particular chuckle fit the description "chortle." There was a delinquent spirit in the tone.

I shook my head and she saw my displeasure.

"Oh. Oh. Some of your best friends are," she said, shrugging, smirking.

"And even if that wasn't true…" I said.

She'd left her coat over a chair. She was tugging the cap off the huge scotch bottle. I told her that I had scotch open, but she waved my offer away, saying she had her own flask, too, but this was for us.

She'd remembered that when we were together I'd liked Dewar's.

As Pat poured herself some Dewar's, she said, "Tell me, do your Jewish friends dance the 'holly, holly cost'?"

She laughed again, and I realized she was not just a little drunk. She was smashed.

In three hours twelve women were arriving to meet her, members of a professional artists and writers group I was hosting that night.

What we do in the group is first listen to the latest chapters or stories from the writers, then the artists display what they have brought. The writers talk a lot about agents and publishers, the artists about galleries and collectors. We have been meeting for twenty years, once a month at each other's homes or studios.

While Pat sat at the kitchen table, I made her a grilled cheese sandwich. To get her off the subject of the Jews I asked her how things had gone at her uncle's ranch. She was starting to answer when she was suddenly interrupted.

I had a Siamese cat, "ER," named for Eleanor Roosevelt. She slept upstairs with a Persian and a tiger, and when anyone came to the house, she sauntered downstairs to greet whoever it was. I always imagined her saying to the others, "*I'll* go down."

ER leapt from the floor to the kitchen table, delighting Pat.

I remembered Pat calling one of my Siamese "Mr. Shvartz!" with a Yiddish accent, way back, long, long ago…. But it had never bothered me then. He had been named Mr. Schwartz for a Madison Avenue butcher who often threw treats into the meat order for my cats.

In the '50s we all told jokes that would be labeled politically incorrect now, and most of us didn't know the subtleties of what would decades later be considered offensive language and attitude, or politically incorrect. I remembered my friend Tom's jokes about Izzy and Sammy.

"Will you take a nap with me, ER?" Pat said to the cat. "I bet you wish you could have some ham, too."

"Yes, you could probably use a nap," I said.

"You got me to like Siamese," she said. "I remember one night you met me at LaGuardia—I'd just come home from visiting my mother. We went to your place on 13th Street. My cat Spider was sitting in your apartment house windows with all your Siamese. Do you remember that night?"

"Yes, I do."

"No reason why you should, of course."

The night she was remembering was when she gave me the gold wedding band engraved *rememb*. In the '70s, my apartment in Brooklyn Heights had been burgled, and whatever jewelry I wasn't wearing had been taken. I never wore it after Pat and I split, but I was fond of it. It reminded me of the good times we'd had before we moved to Pennsylvania. I thought this is the way it *should* go: easy reminiscences, a friendliness, as we caught up with each other, but as she might put it I couldn't "get past" her opening remarks. I felt disgusted by them, and physically distressed as though I'd eaten spoiled food and would pay soon. Maybe we *both* needed naps. I showed her the downstairs guestroom and went up to my room, but I wasn't able to rest, much less sleep. I was worried that she'd drink too much, that she'd embarrass me in front of my group by saying something bigoted and gauche.

iii

Before everyone arrived, Pat insisted that the enormous bottle of Dewar's she'd brought from Kennedy Airport be placed back on the kitchen table. While she was napping I'd exchanged it for my own half-empty bottle of J & B. Symbolically, I suppose, *she* was going to buy the drinks. I think she felt freer drinking all she wanted from a bottle she'd supplied than from one half-full house bottle.

She had showered and dressed the same way she had every evening when we were living in Bucks County, Pennsylvania. Neatly pressed flannel pants, the ubiquitous white shirt with an ascot, her blue gabardine blazer, and loafers freshly shined.

The nap seemed to have sobered her up, to the point of appearing a bit defended. She muttered something about her trip from Fort Worth being tiresome, to say nothing of the tedium involved in visiting family. She said *People* magazine came down while she was there, photographed her, and did half of an interview. They'd be calling so that they could finish it.

"I don't like to go down there," she said. "It brings back memories of my mother." She was pouring herself a glass of scotch. I had wine out on the table, too, with the bottled water and Cokes. But only a few of the women coming drank. Everyone had to drive home, most at least ten miles from my house. Three came from Shelter Island, which involved a trip to Sag Harbor and a ride on the ferry.

"Take it easy," I said, watching the whiskey rise. "It'll be a long evening."

"What do they drink? Wine?"

"If that."

"What kind of artists and writers are *they?*" she asked.

"Old ones," I said.

She laughed. "We *do* slow down," she said. Then she blurted out, "I even had lung cancer." She had a Gitanes lit, resting in the ashtray.

"I didn't know that."

"How could you? I didn't tell anyone. It cost me a fortune! I got absolutely no benefits from *any* country, after all the taxes I paid, too! Nothing!"

"If it'll help that I don't smoke, so *you* won't, I don't need to. Let's not smoke."

She shrugged. "I'll cut down. It's just the excitement of arriving here. Anyway, I'm going to go when I go. This will probably be my last trip over here."

"I don't think the women in this group are crazy about anyone smoking. I don't usually smoke around them."

Pat shrugged again. "So I'll come out here when I want to smoke."

"Fine."

"I'm not going to be any trouble."

"I know that, Pat," I lied. I didn't know what to expect of the evening. I remembered that in the old days I would not know Pat was drunk until she said something either outlandish or completely out-of-context. I said, "I'm sorry to hear about the cancer."

"So am I. But my mother lived until she was ninety-six, completely out of it for years. My cousin Dan had to drive some twenty-five miles to Fort Worth every week, checking on her diaper supply, and he's in his eighties!... Do you need help?"

"No, thanks." I was remembering the four-page single spaced typewritten letter her mother'd written me when we broke up, saying how sorry she was and detailing everything that was wrong with Pat's women.

Mary Highsmith was a high-strung, jealous, and possessive woman. It always struck me that the two of them enjoyed a certain folie à deux back in the '50s.

"It always depresses me to go home," Pat said. "It makes me think of what might have been, if my mother hadn't been so cruel."

"Why did you dedicate two books to her?"

"I was trying to impress her, I suppose. There wasn't any way to do it. She always found fault."

She shrugged and changed the subject. "Are all these women straight?"

"All are."

"Do they know you're not?"

"Yes."

"How do they feel about it?"

"I don't think they care one way or the other," I said.

"Sometimes I think I liked it better when we had to sneak around."

"I think of that sometimes, too. All the subterfuge. It was like a game."

"I remember when Betty and Olive lived in Sneden's and kept a timer in their guest bedroom, did I tell you that?" Pat guffawed. "Every night the guestroom lights went off promptly at ten. If the neighbors *were* watching, they must have wondered who the martinet was, Betty or Olive."

I was laughing, too. I hadn't thought of that in a long time.

"Yes, they rigged that up so the neighbors wouldn't know they shared a bedroom."

I almost regretted inviting the women to meet at my house that night. It might have been easier if we just spent time together, reminiscing. It seemed as though she was warming up a bit, recalling the old days.

I told her one reason I'd invited the group was that I thought it would appeal to her, since she had always been torn between wanting to be an artist or a writer.

"If I could have made a living as an artist, I would have," she said.

She shook her head and sighed. "That was another thing." Then she was silent.

"What was another thing?"

"My mother never had a good word for my art. I was better than she was, too, only when I was younger I didn't know that."

"She was a crazy woman, Pat. You have to think of it that way."

"But she *was* my mother."

"And you were an only child."

"That was the whole problem. I would have liked it if I'd had a sibling to help pay for her all those years she vegetated."

She poured another scotch.

But who was counting?

Everyone wanted Pat to go first when the artists began their talking, since she'd announced she wanted to be in that category. I decided to just let her be herself, for I had an idea she would be anyway.

She was drinking scotch neat by that time, and had a sort of goony grin on her face.

"This is my house," she said. She was passing around photographs of a very severe-appearing, fort-like house.

"I designed it myself, which I hope qualifies me as an artist, since I don't have my sketchbooks with me. I had help from a prominent architect whose name probably isn't familiar here."

"Is he Swiss?" someone asked.

"Yes," and she said his name, without anyone's appearing to know him. "But I did the designing," she insisted. "I told him what I wanted."

The windows seemed like lookout slits in the side of an old fort.

"And more art here," Pat said, and there were pictures of a young woman, smiling, pretty. Pat said. "German girl." She gave me a smile. "Good looking, huh?"

"Yes. Good looking."

"If I had to choose between the girl and the house, I'd choose the house," Pat said.

Now, everyone was laughing with her.

They were also aware of her leaving them regularly to fill her glass and have a smoke in the kitchen. She had brought a carton of Merit lights, as well as Gitanes, alternating between them. That was probably her concession to cancer.

The four artists made their presentations, followed by two writers. Pat listened attentively. Then someone asked Pat if she would mind telling us what made her write mysteries rather than regular novels.

"It's the American publishers that try to categorize me," she said. "I am not a mystery writer. I am a writer. Americans put 'a novel of suspense' on my book jackets, but my European publishers prefer not to label me."

Pat was still able to pack it away without a physical reaction. I never heard her thick-tongued nor saw her stagger. She was all smiles, seeming to genuinely enjoy the evening. I think my guests enjoyed her, too.

The moment after everyone had left, she said, "Let me make us nightcaps."

We went into the den and sat down.

"That tall artist with the white hair and the big nose," Pat said. "A Jewess?"

"No, she's French."

"She could be a French Jewess."

"Yes, but she's not. What difference does it make?"

"None to you," Pat said. "You love all Jews."

"I don't love all *any* group. Do you hate all Jews?"

"You see, it's a matter of propinquity. You live near New York. That makes you a Jew lover. Where I live we don't take to them. I don't know any Swiss or French or anyone where I live who is sympathetic to Jews. On the contrary!"

"Okay," I said. "I think you've made your point."

"Your little group is all right," she said. "I don't go in for that sort of thing. There isn't any opportunity where I live for that sort of thing, anyway. My life is not socially active nor chic."

"Do you have friends in your town?"

"One or two. I go to the movies in Locarno with Ingebord, who speaks German. I have a couple for dinner sometimes. But I'm not interested in socializing.... I keep in touch with a lot of people. I write letters."

"I know. You're a good correspondent."

"I write Paul Bowles, Gore Vidal, Julian Symonds—you'd be surprised."

"I'm not surprised."

"And they write back. I write Peter Ustinov. He can't type, even, and has no intention of learning."

"Tell me what you remember about *us*," I said.

She didn't need time to think.

"You held nothing back," she said. "You said everything you thought."

"Yes. That was and probably still is a big fault."

"It wasn't right," she said shaking her head. "Words once spoken hurt the most." She sighed. "It was so hard, so hard."

I was reminded of an inscription she wrote in *A Game for the Living* after we'd been dating awhile:

Many things are hard, just not the right things. Do think this over. Love, Pat. April 1, 1960.

I never knew the context.

"I've been thinking a lot about my old lovers," she said, "most of whom are dead now. They were an interesting lot, none of them alike."

"Did you keep in touch with them?"

"Not any from the fifties and sixties. But I wanted to look *you* up. If you could have moved to Europe with me, we might have lasted."

"I don't think location had that much to do with it. I think we moved in together too fast."

"You're right about that. And maybe we should never have lived together. That kills things between people."

"I wanted to get you off in the sticks where no one would steal you away."

"It's always the jealous one who leaves first," said Pat. "You ran off with that Jewess who called herself Gus."

"Well, her name is August. We're still friends," I said. "She was Pennsylvania Dutch, not Jewish."

"We probably *wouldn't* have lasted," said Pat. "We were most compatible physically, but otherwise we disappointed each other, or you were disappointed in me for whatever reason."

It was almost midnight.

Pat stood up. "I don't stay up this late at home," she said. "Not ever."

"You can sleep late tomorrow."

"I get up early. That's all right. You don't have to make me breakfast or fuss."

"We'll go out for lunch, okay?" I said. "I'll show you some of the Hamptons."

"I've been here before," she said. "I stayed with Charles Latimer on Skimhampton Road. Do you know him?"

She had never mentioned that in her letters. I said I didn't know him and she said he was a friend, but he was in Florida now.

"I do have friends," she said. "It's just that we write more than we see each other because we live all over the place."

Pat had lived "all over the place," too. She had "settled" in England, then Italy, then several villages in France, and at the end she had moved twice in Switzerland. Her wanderlust had never left her.

I told her to leave her door open if she wanted a cat for company. I had four at the time and two dogs.

In bed, I tossed and turned, thinking how differently I'd imagined our reunion. For one thing, her illness took some of the edge off her bigotry. I couldn't juggle sympathy and disgust very successfully. For another, I was disappointed that we couldn't seriously discuss Israel and Palestine. In the early '50s I had a friend who was in love with Enayat, a young student from Jordan. He was here studying dentistry, working as well, and sending all the money he could spare to his relatives in Palestine. We often discussed the Israel/Palestine problem, and Enayat pointed out to me the transgressions resulting from the 1948 land grab, which left everyone he was close to, and himself, homeless. He had enlightened me early on about the injustice done to Palestinians.

I had learned just enough from Enayat to imagine I'd be interested in discussing Pat's position, but it didn't take long to realize Israel was less pertinent to the subject than her hatred of all Jews. I also realized it was the one topic I should steer clear of, for it triggered impassioned harangues, narrowed eyes, and another jolt of whatever she was drinking.

I finally took an Ambien to sleep.

iv

The next day I took her to Spots in Sag Harbor. It was a small luncheonette filled with books and art by locals. It was a little like a tea room, mostly sandwiches and salads, no liquor license. I had to ask the owners if it was okay for Pat to bring a few bottles of beer in a paper bag. It turned out that they were great fans of hers, and thrilled that she was there. She could have brought in anything she wanted to.

I was right to think she'd like the big yellow and green parrot they kept there. Alex seldom spoke or came down from his perch to notice customers but he did for Pat. He said "Hello" and "So long" and hopped about as she talked to him. She said she wasn't very hungry. I suspected she had quenched her appetite while she was waiting for me to get up that morning. Although she ordered a medium hamburger, she left half of it.

After, we stopped by Canio's bookstore. He was a bookseller I greatly admired, specializing in used and new books. He had always been good to writers, staging readings in his small shop, featuring all the locals, famous and unknown.

I thought he would like meeting Pat, and she might be interested in his rickety wooden store, bulging mostly with used books, then books by the natives, and finally a few quality books: poems by Cavafy, the new Philip Roth, the collected works of Frank O'Hara, an Elizabeth Jolley, a José Donoso, on and on. She was uninterested, stood with her hands in her pockets. Then Canio asked her to sign what books of hers he had in stock. She agreed, saying nothing, but the look on her face spoke for her.

"They all want to make money off you," she grumbled as we drove away. "I've been fending off would-be biographers. I've had a couple of persistent ones, very annoying. I tell them wait till I'm dead. It's all for money. They neither know me nor particularly like me, they just smell money as a buzzard smells dead fish!"

That night we had dinner with two old friends of mine at Della Femina's, a restaurant nearby. I'd told Pat that one of them had written a novel, and she'd looked at it before we left the house. Pat had a martini while she studied the menu. I should have picked a less fancy place, but I knew we'd drink and I didn't want to drive too far. There they served things like yellowfin tuna with kimchi and soba noodles, the kind of food I wasn't fond of, and I knew Pat wouldn't be. She wondered if it was possible to get a steak and frites or maybe scrambled eggs. She said, "Yes, scrambled eggs, bacon, red wine." The waiter said they could not fix eggs for her; she had to stick to the menu. Suddenly she was not interested in wine, either, and finally settled for some chicken she scraped the sauce off of, a green salad, and a Heineken. Pat made no attempt at casual conversation. She answered questions about her novels, but did not ask either friend a question, not even the fledgling novelist.

Soon her focus was on a table of blacks, three men and a woman, at the end of the room.

"That's something I don't see a lot of in my town," she said. "Oh, you do in big cities of Europe, but I had the idea this small town was mostly white."

Next Pat said that blacks were incapable of thinking ahead, of figuring out that sexual intercourse may lead to pregnancy, and that if you spend your pay on Friday, there's none by next Wednesday.

My friends kept their heads bent over their food.

Pat continued. She said that black men got physically ill if they didn't have sexual intercourse many times a month.

I groaned and Pat said, "Marijane thinks I make things up. She thinks I'm this prejudiced monster.... When I was six in 1927 I started school in New York City public schools. I was delighted to see a few blacks in my class. We had the same accent because I'd lived in Texas. We were pals on the playing field. Is it Old Whitey's fault if they don't stay in school?"

"Why did you choose to live abroad?" one of my friends asked, changing the subject.

"Because I'm more compatible with Europeans," said Pat. "They've always understood me better. When I wrote

Strangers on a Train, my first book, which I called *Criss Cross,* it was turned down by six publishers before Harper and Brothers took it in 1950. Then Alfred Hitchcock made it into a film and got all the credit. But when the European directors like René Clement, Claude Chabrol, Michel Deville, and the rest made one of my books into a film, *I* got credit, not them, or at least I was equal to them.... I *sell* in Europe, too. Here a book I wrote in 1986 called *Found in the Street,* and set in New York, sold only four thousand copies. It sold forty thousand in Germany!"

She ate very little again, but polished off six Heinekens and on the drive home asked me if I wasn't proud of her for not saying what she thought about Jews.

"Are you proud of yourself?"

She said, "When we were talking about Yaddo, and I was saying I thought I might leave my money there, I didn't tell them that I was making inquiries to learn if I could leave some to the Intifadeh."

"Did you think that would shock them?"

"Wouldn't it? It shocks you, doesn't it?"

"No, because it doesn't come as a surprise now that you've been here a while, and I've listened to you."

"Do you still keep a record of conversations?"

"Some."

"We'll have a nightcap and I'll tell you how I feel about the Jews," she said. "For the record.... I quite like having drinks after dinner. I remember we used to save some wine for after dinner when we lived together, and we'd sit by the fire and talk. There's none of that where I live now."

"What about other people you've lived with?"

"I keep telling you: Since 1961 I didn't even try to live with anyone. For one thing, I can't do creative work with anyone else in the house. I've had several relationships since, of course. It's a mistake young people make (though I wasn't young in 1960) to try to live with the person they're in love with. This ruins everything, rather pronto, too."

I had a bottle of Rémy Martin that hadn't ever been opened. We each poured ourselves a glass and she said, "Put this in your cahier. I was in Yaddo in 1948 when Israel was founded and we were all happy about it. But the Likud Party has done a lot of damage. Irrevocable damage. If you only knew how the Jews are despised where I live!"

"Do you live in some little Nazi coven?"

"I'm not surrounded by neo-Nazis, just easy-going *Ticinesi*, old Italian families, and new families of workers. I notice the products from Israel are shunned in the supermarkets, and the Jaffa orange juice disappeared this year. People say, why should I buy something from that country? And when they know I'm an American they ask me why America gives these people so much money. Everyone knows Israel imprisons without habeas corpus, throws families who are not terrorists out of their houses at gunpoint, with the standing army of Israel right behind them with the guns at the ready.... Don't sigh! I'm telling you the truth! Aren't you interested in the truth?"

"It's late, and I don't want to argue."

"You always used to like to argue. You just don't like to hear that Israel, your favorite country, doesn't give a damn about the Geneva convention!"

"Pat, why can't you drop it? We're not going to be together that long."

"It's okay to say whatever one pleases about the English, the Italians, the French, but watch your words if you say a word against the Jews!"

Pat was too sloshed to let go. "Did I tell you?" she said as I began turning off the lights, "that the Jew editor Otto Penzler removed my dedication *To the Palestinian people* from *People Who Knock on the Door* without a by-your-leave request? Penguin and European countries left it in!"

"Pat, you sound like someone with an obsessive-compulsive disorder. You can't go for long without bringing up the Jews, just as someone has to compulsively wash their hands, or go back three steps."

"Now you sound like your old self," she said. "You could always find some fault I had, always!"

"I don't ever remember you being so bigoted."

"I didn't dare open my mouth. I remember how you thought that Jewish psychologist, Martha Wolfenstein, hung the moon. She wasn't even a medical doctor. Freud, the great Jewish gift to the tormented mind, was a biologist, did you know that? And a cocaine addict! So much for Jewish veracity!"

"Goodnight," I said. "I'm just worn out. I'm sorry."

Pat stood, too. She shrugged. She said, "As you wish." She picked up the brandy snifter and went down the hall to the guest room.

I fell asleep thinking about her asking me if I wasn't "shocked" to hear she would like to leave money to the Intifadeh. I thought of her writing, particularly some of her short story collections: *The Animal Lover's Book of Beastly Murder* (a cat jumps through the cat door with a human finger in its mouth); *Little Tales of Misogyny; Slowly, Slowly*

in the Wind—even the titles had a certain shock value....
And of course, Ripley getting away with murder, always....
I had never thought of Pat as a show-off, or as someone
seeking attention with her own shock treatment, but that
seemed to now be a part of her modus operandi.

V

Again, I slept as late as I could, and we went for lunch. Pat
said that while I was sleeping she'd looked over my books.

"I remember when you still hadn't even written *Sudden
Endings*," she said, referring to my nonfiction study of
famous suicides, published by Doubleday in 1964. "I read
some of it, you know. I liked the story of Hart Crane. The
way he was bullied by his father. Typical parental abuse!"

"And *you* got *Janus* published eventually, too."

"As *The Two Faces of January*," Pat said. 'What a ridicu-
lous title! I did a lot of rewrite on that. It was never my
favorite book, and I probably wouldn't have worked on it,
but I wanted to prove Joan Kahn wrong. She didn't think it
could be salvaged."

"I remember."

"Remember? Christ, what a little dictator she was!
That whole family of Jews thought they were God's gift
to publishing...like so many of that tribe."

"Let's get some lunch. Please, let's GET OFF the subject
of the Jews."

"You can't bribe me with a hot dog to forget their
treachery!" she muttered.

"Tell me what you're working on." We were in the car now.

"You know I don't talk about work-in-progress," she
said. 'But I'll say this. Remember you sent me that guide to

gay places in Europe? Remember they had a capital *G* by male bars and a small *g* by female? I went to one of the bars in Zurich. I took a friend. It was nothing exciting particularly but that's a good title. *Small g.*"

"Yes, it is."

"And everyone's waiting for me to do a lesbian book since I was so successful with Claire Morgan, so I think I'll do it."

We lunched at a pub in Montauk and drove around talking about writing, which was always a safe subject with us. We talked more about her mother, too. Although Pat had deliberately cut off all contact with her mother in the 1970s, Mary Highsmith was never far from her mind, particularly as Pat looked back on her life, which seemed to be the hidden agenda during this visit to her homeland, possibly for the last time. Pat's bitterness over her relationship with her mother was almost as relentless as her fury at the Jews.

I wanted to ask her why she'd never put her thoughts about Israel and the Arabs into her books, but I didn't dare broach that subject, which miraculously she hadn't brought up herself in at least an hour. She had promised to speak that night to the Ashawagh Hall Writer's Workshop, of which I was the founder. We benefit the Springs Scholarship Fund and we'd been meeting on Thursday nights for eighteen years.

Pat always took some cold beers along when we went anywhere, for fear we'd stop someplace that didn't serve it. So by the time we got back to my house, she'd had a few, to go with the double martini at lunch, and she was ready for a nap before class.

No one missed the Ashawagh Hall Writer's Workshop that night. I knew Pat would like our meeting place, which is a dusty old attic in a small community center, a few blocks from my house There, in the downstairs, various organizations meet, and art shows are held, but we writers are the only ones to use the upstairs. We have a huge table, with two dozen chairs around it, all filled that night, all eager to hear Pat.

I handed my camera to a young man and told him Pat had given permission for him to shoot freely as she spoke. I had asked her, dreading the response, but—ever unpredictable—she had said to go ahead, with a shrug. "Do what you have to do," she added. I did interfere when class was over and a few individuals stepped up to pose with her, her face frowning with discomfort.

But before that she was all smiles, and she did not disappoint them. She told how she got ideas and how she turned them into novels, and she also told them mistakes she had made so that characters or situations didn't work. She took questions as we went along. She said that she got up early and wrote mornings, had lunch and a nap, and saved afternoons for yard work, carpentry, or art work, evenings for reading and writing letters. She said she lived in Europe because she was treated better there, and paid more there: that she also preferred the food and wine there, and she had a love of languages.

There was not a word about Jews or Arabs or blacks, and at the end she received loud applause and some of the writers even stood and cried, "Brava!"

She was pleased, I could tell, and tired, so I made her corned beef hash with an egg on top, which used to be a favorite supper. I told her she would have been a good teacher, and she said a book she'd written twenty years ago called *Plotting and Writing Suspense Fiction* had sold very well here and in Great Britain.

We both felt good about the evening. I decided we should quit while we were ahead. She agreed. She said she was really tired, and that she smoked too much when we drank and talked after dinner.

She was to leave the next day near noon. She was to do a morning interview with *People* magazine, so she agreed to answer the phone. I slept late again, and again she fixed her own coffee. She had some juice, and made no attempt to hide my bottle of Absolut, which she'd placed on the kitchen table.

She said, "I took the liberty of getting all my books out of your bookcase and autographing them. I'd already written in a few of the old ones, I see."

"Yes. Well, thanks, Pat. How did the interview with *People* go?"

"The person who interviewed me didn't know my work at all, so I don't have great hopes for it."

She was playing with a switchblade, of all things, and, knowing Pat's frugal side, I'm sure it was the same one she used to wield in Bucks County, as she tended her plants. Now she was passing it from hand to hand and then turning it one way and another on the table.

"I won't do this if it makes you nervous," she said.

"I don't know why you're doing it," I said. But I knew why. She had been drinking a bit of vodka. I knew the tone, the hooded look in her eyes, and then as she spoke again the same old same old.

She said, "The Arab–Israeli business goes back to human rights, for me. I don't think some people are created more equal than others, and I like the idea that a man's home is his castle, however humble. This country finances so much of Israel's activities, settlements, wars—and the dear old Jewish press—start with the *New York Times*—has the whole U.S. of A. seaboard mesmerized. No comments against Jews, Israeli policy, or you're anti-Semitic."

"You can be as pro-Palestine and as anti-Israel as you want," I said. "What I find annoying is your hatred of the individual Jew, whether he lives in Jerusalem or down the street."

"Oh the poor, poor heebee jeebies," she whined.

I was ready to blow. I'd managed to hold back for almost three days but I was at the breaking point. I told her Sean would be there in twenty minutes to take her to the airport.

She pushed the button so that the blade of the knife was exposed. "It's really interesting," she said, "that you just refuse to listen to my side."

"I'm going to take a shower," I said. "I had a roll of film out here on the table. Did you see it?"

"Did you use it all up?"

"Yes."

"I haven't seen it."

I left the room, went upstairs, and took a quick shower. I was dressing when I heard Sean beep the horn in the driveway.

I went down and helped Pat with her luggage: a garment bag, a shoulder bag, and a large canvas bag. There was an awkward embrace, and mumbled "Take care of yourselves" and "Good-byes."

When the airport limo was out of my driveway I went inside to both bathrooms, and threw away all the soap.

She wrote a cordial letter of thanks, which I answered in late November, telling her I hoped she would be "uncharacteristically merry for the holidays, and in the New Year, find some peace."

There were a few more letters from her, and then she wrote another on Hotel zum Storchen stationery. She was in Tegna, and it was August 1993.

> *I had a rough month, so my typing of* Small g *did not go as fast as I'd hoped. Had a few nosebleeds, in fact I have not enough "platelets" which have to do with coagulation. So the doctor here is trying to find out why. Most annoying if a nosebleed keeps one awake all night or most of it.... My latest short story sale: a 9-pager to* Sueddeutsche Zeitung *(Munich). Their mag. section had a project. 4 writers participated, among them Joseph Brodsky, and a Russian woman. Mine is about 2 teen-aged boys, NYC, who easily murder a stranger by knocking on a hotel room door. And get away with it.... Best love to you and good health and best to the animals and ER.*
>
> *PAT*
>
> *P.S. USA could save 11 million per day if they would cut the dough to Israel. The Jewish vote is 1%.*

I didn't answer the letter.

The last word from Pat Highsmith was enclosed with photographs of an old dinner party I'd given in summer 1992. She had helped herself to the roll of film she'd told me she hadn't seen, the one I searched everywhere for after she left East Hampton. There were a few of Pat and me together during her visit. I noticed some of the numbered negatives were missing, and surmised they were the ones of her and Sean, and the ones she'd given me permission to take at the writer's workshop.

> *19 Nov. 1994*
> *Just got this surprise package developed. I think they might be of more interest to you than to me. With good wishes and love, as ever, Pat.*

Pat died February 1995.

I remember when we spoke of our wills and possibly leaving money to friends, Pat said most of her friends were her age or older, that if she left them any money, their "greedy" relatives would get it. When I pointed out that I had found ways to leave money "conditionally," to my older friends, she replied that she owed everything to Yaddo. That was very far from the truth, for she had been at this elite writer's colony only a few months in 1948. Her admission there was before she was famous; it was promoted by Truman Capote, who wanted to lease her apartment for a short time…. Nevertheless, Yaddo would be her sole beneficiary, and several old, expectant friends would ultimately be disappointed.

Her memorial service was held in the church of Tegna, Ticino, Switzerland.

The invitation from Diogenes was printed both in English and in German. Pat would have liked that.

About the Author

MARIJANE MEAKER was one of the early '50s paper-back writers. She wrote twenty-two books under the pseudonyms Vin Packer and Ann Aldrich. Under her own name, she has written a nonfiction study of famous suicides and six novels including *Shockproof Sydney Skate*. As the young adult novelist, M. E. Kerr, she has written twenty-five books, her latest called *Snakes Don't Miss Their Mothers*. Ms. Meaker lives in East Hampton, New York.